# Beta
# Mathema...

## New Edition

Compiled by
**T. R. Goddard,**
**J. W. Adams and R. P. Beaumont**

 **Schofield & Sims Ltd Huddersfield**

0 7217 2260 1

First printed 1979

Reprinted 1979 (twice)

Reprinted 1980 (twice)

Reprinted 1981

Reprinted 1982

Reprinted 1983

Revised and reprinted 1985

Reprinted 1986, 1989, 1990, 1991, 1992, 1994, 1996

The books in the two series forming this programme comprise:

Ready for Alpha and Beta  0 7217 2266 0

| | |
|---|---|
| Beta Mathematics 1<br>0 7217 2258 X | Alpha Mathematics 1<br>0 7217 2250 4 |
| Beta Mathematics 2<br>0 7217 2259 8 | Alpha Mathematics 2<br>0 7217 2251 2 |
| Beta Mathematics 3<br>0 7217 2260 1 | Alpha Mathematics 3<br>0 7217 2252 0 |
| Beta Mathematics 4<br>0 7217 2261 X | Alpha Mathematics 4<br>0 7217 2253 9 |

Printed in England by The Amadeus Press Ltd, Huddersfield

# Number products, factors, square numbers

**A**

| 13 | 42 | 36 | 24 | 30 | 40 |
|----|----|----|----|----|----|
| | 56 | 72 | 14 | 9 | 16 |

Which number in the box is the product of

1  5 and 8       2  9 and 8       3  4 and 9
4  7 and 6       5  10 and 3      6  2 and 7?

The product of 4 and 6 is 24.
24 is called a **multiple** of 4.
It is also a **multiple** of 6.

7

| 12 | 16 | 20 | 24 | 18 |
|----|----|----|----|----|
| | 32 | 36 | 42 | 28 |

Which of the numbers in the box are multiples of
   a  4       b  6       c  4 and 6?

8  Write the set of multiples of 4 from 4 to 40.

9  Write the set of multiples of 6 from 6 to 60.

10  Find two multiples of 4 which are greater than 80 but less than 90.

11  Find three multiples of 6 which are greater than 120 but less than 140.

12  Complete the following sets.
Multiples of 5
5, □, □, □, □, □, □, □, □, 50
Multiples of 8
8, □, □, □, □, □, □, □, □, 80
Multiples of 7
7, □, □, □, □, □, □, □, □, 70

13  Write the multiples of
   a  9 from 9 to 90   b  10 from 10 to 100.

The **factors** of 6 are 1, 2, 3 and 6.

14  Write a sentence telling what a **factor** is.

15  Draw this table and fill in the missing factor or product.

| factor | 9 | | 8 | | 6 |
|--------|---|---|---|---|---|
| factor | 8 | 7 | | 6 | 9 |
| product | | 63 | 80 | 42 | |

Find the different factors of each of these numbers. Omit 1 and the number itself.

16  18     17  24     18  16     19  36     20  40

**B**  A **prime number** has only two factors, 1 and the number itself.
3 is a prime number, 1 and 3 are its only factors.

1  Write the set of prime numbers from 1 to 20.

2  Give a reason why no even number, except 2, is a prime number.

3

| 21 | 35 | 29 | 37 | 33 | 41 |
|----|----|----|----|----|----|
| | 55 | 43 | 27 | 49 | |

Which of the numbers in the box are prime numbers?

**Square numbers**

1

2 groups of 2
$2 \times 2$

3 groups of 3
$3 \times 3$

$2 \times 2$ is read as 2 squared.
It is written as $2^2$.
Write and complete:

4  3 squared $= 3 \times 3 = 3^2 = \square$

5  4 squared $= 4 \times 4 = 4^2 = \square$.

6  Write in full $1^2$. Find the value of $1^2$.

7  On squared paper draw a diagram to show $5^2$. Write underneath the diagram $5^2 = 5 \times 5 = \square$.

8  Find the value of
   a  $6^2$     b  $8^2$     c  $10^2$     d  $20^2$.

9  Notice that all square numbers have two factors which are the same.
Write the missing numbers.
   a  $49 = \square^2$     b  $81 = \square^2$     c  $100 = \square^2$

10  On squared paper draw and complete this 100 multiplication square.

| X | 1 | 2 | 3 | 4 | 5 | 6 | 7 | 8 | 9 | 10 |
|---|---|---|---|---|---|---|---|---|---|----|
| 1 | ① | 2 | 3 | 4 | 5 | 6 | 7 | 8 | 9 | 10 |
| 2 | 2 | ④ | 6 | 8 | 10 | 12 | 14 | 16 | 18 | 20 |
| 3 | 3 | 6 | 9 | 12 | 15 | 18 | 21 | 24 | 27 | 30 |

Ring all the square numbers.
Describe the pattern you have made.

# Sets

A **set** is a group or collection of things which are alike in some way.
Each thing shown in a set is called a **member** of the set.

## A

1  In the diagram marked C, there is a group
of counters enclosed in a ring.
It is a **set** of counters.
   a  How many counters are there?
   b  Write and complete:
      C is a set of _____ with ☐ members.

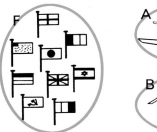

2  Write and complete the following for
each of these sets.
F is a set of _____ with ☐ members.
A is a set of _____ with ☐ members.
B is a set of _____ with ☐ members.

In each set, C, F, A and B, the members
are alike in some way.

## B

1  In the set S, all the members of the set
are shapes.
   a  How many members are there in the set?
   b  Write and complete:
      Set S is a set of _____ with ☐ members.

2  In the same way, write a name which
describes each of the sets L, F and T.
Give the number of members in each set.

3  Draw and complete the set of coins
less than £1. You can call it set M.
How many members are there in the set?

4  In the same way, draw the set of
   a  the bronze coins
   b  the cupro-nickel coins.

## C

Words, letters or numbers may be members of sets.
1  Describe in words each of the sets A, L and N. Give the number of members in each set.

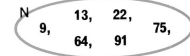

Show the following sets. Put each set in
a box or draw a ring round it.
2  the set of numbers on a clock face
3  the set of days in a week
4  the set of letters called vowels
5  the set of numbers on a die
6  the set of people in your family
7  Write the number of members in each
of the sets **2** to **6**.

Write the members of each of the
following sets.
You are told the number in each.
8  a set of pets with four members
9  a set of even numbers with five members
10  a set of odd numbers with six members
11  a set of triangles with three members
12  Why are you told how many members to
write in examples **8** to **11**?

# Sets

## A  Naming and writing sets

You have been showing the members of a set by putting them in a box or drawing a ring round them.

Usually **brackets** { } are used to enclose them.

The brackets mean 'the set of'.

A capital letter is used to name the set.

Set T is a set of garden tools with four members, shown by drawings. They are enclosed in a box.

T = {spade, trowel, fork, rake}
or T = the set of spade, trowel, fork, rake

1  This set is named M, which stands for motor vehicles. There are four members. Write and complete:
M = {_____, _____, _____, _____}
or M = the set of _____, _____, _____, _____.

2  L = {a, b, c, d, e}
Write and complete:
L is the set of the first ☐ letters in the alphabet.

3  N = {1, 2, 3, 4, 5, 6, 7}
Write and complete:
N = the set of the _____ ☐ whole numbers.

**Remember**  A comma separates the members of a set.

Name with a capital letter and write the members of these sets in brackets.

4  a set of five pets

5  a set of four vegetables

6  a set of six trees

7  a set of two shapes with four sides

8  a set of three British Kings

9  the set of the months of the year with 30 days

10  the set of even numbers between 5 and 21

11  the set of odd numbers between 36 and 52

12  the set of letters in your surname (letters should not be written twice)

13  the set of forenames of the members in your family

14  the set of numbers between 2 and 10 which are factors of 12

15  the set of the product of 5 and 4

## B

1  Write two more members for each of the following sets.
C = {red, blue, green, _____, _____}
B = {arm, leg, toe, _____, _____}
N = {10, 50, 30 _____, _____}
F = {$\frac{5}{5}$, $\frac{2}{2}$, $\frac{3}{3}$, _____, _____}
R = {I, II, III, IV, _____, _____}
V = {a, e, i, _____, _____}

2  The members of the four sets T, R, F and S below have been mixed up.
8, 27, 55, 9, 4, 7, 16, 49, 22, 35
Using the numbers above only, write these sets.
T = {numbers of which 2 is a factor}
R = {numbers of which 3 is a factor}
F = {numbers of which 5 is a factor}
S = {numbers of which 7 is a factor}

# Sets

**A** The names and ages in years of the children in the School Art Club are given in the table.

| Age 9 years | Age 10 years |
|---|---|
| Freda<br>Alison<br>John | Alan<br>Jill<br>Charles<br>Joan<br>Tim |

| Age 11 years | Age 12 years |
|---|---|
| Carole<br>Julie<br>Paul<br>Tony<br>Sarah<br>Alec | |

1 Write in brackets the members of each of these sets.
A = {9 year-old children}
B = {10 year-old children}
C = {11 year-old children}
D = {12 year-old children}

2 How many members are there in set A, set B, set C?

3 How many members are there in {children in the Art Club}?

In set D there are no members. It is an **empty** set, which is shown as { } or by using the sign ∅ e.g.
Set D = { } or ∅.

4 Some of the following are empty sets. Pick them out and write them in two ways.
e.g. B = {boys 3 metres tall}
B = { } or B = ∅

D = {days of the week beginning with D}
T = {teachers 5 m tall}
S = {squares with three sides}
G = {houses with green doors}
A = {triangles with three acute angles}
F = {fractions greater than $\frac{3}{4}$}

**B** Some sets have one member or just a few members.

1 Write the members of each of these sets.
S = {multiples of both 3 and 4 less than 20}
B = {multiples of 7 between 30 and 50}
F = {factors of 24 omitting 1 and 24}

Some sets have many members. e.g.
C = {children who attend your school}
E = {whole numbers less than 500}
Write a set which has

2 no members     3 one member only

4 a few members     5 many members.

There is a short way of writing sets with a large number of members. e.g.
P = {1, 2, 3, . . . 14, 15, 16}

The three dots stand for
4, 5, 6, 7, 8, 9, 10, 11, 12, 13,

What do the dots stand for in these sets?

6 A = {a, b, c, . . . x, y, z}

7 M = {7, 14, 21, . . . 70, 77, 84}

8 F = {$5\frac{1}{2}$, 6, $6\frac{1}{2}$, . . . 12, $12\frac{1}{2}$, 13}

9 Using dots, write the members of these sets.
N = {page numbers in this book}
E = {multiples of 8 less than 100}
T = {numbers less than 40 divisible by 3}

In some sets, the list of members goes on and on, there is no end. e.g.
O = {all odd numbers}
O = {1, 3, 5, . . .}

The three dots are placed at the end after the first few members have been shown.

10 Using dots, write the members of these sets.
E = {all even numbers}
O = {odd numbers greater than 100}
M = {multiples of 10}
N = {whole numbers greater than 1000}
H = {multiples of 100}

# Fractions

## A

The fraction of the whole one which is shaded is **one-fourth** $\frac{1}{4}$ or **one-quarter**.

What fraction of each of these whole ones is shaded?
Write the answers in words and figures.

These are the answers in figures.

$$\frac{1}{3} \qquad \frac{1}{5} \qquad \frac{1}{8}$$

> The number **below** the line in each fraction shows into how many equal parts each whole one is divided.
>
> The number gives the name to the fraction and is called the **denominator** of the fraction.

Write in words and figures the fraction of each whole one which is shaded.

7  What is the denominator of each fraction? What does the denominator tell you?

8  A cake is shared equally among 7 children. What fraction of the cake does each child receive? Answer in words and figures.

9  A length of string is cut into 9 equal pieces.
What fraction of the length is each piece?

10  A quantity of nuts was packed into 20 equal bags.
What fraction of the nuts was put into each bag?

11  Arrange these fractions in order, putting the largest first.

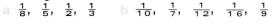
a  $\frac{1}{8}$, $\frac{1}{5}$, $\frac{1}{2}$, $\frac{1}{3}$    b  $\frac{1}{10}$, $\frac{1}{7}$, $\frac{1}{12}$, $\frac{1}{16}$, $\frac{1}{9}$

## B

The fraction of the whole one which is shaded is **three-fourths** $\frac{3}{4}$ or **three-quarters**.

What fraction of each of these whole ones is shaded?
Write the answers in words and figures.

These are the answers in figures.

$$\frac{2}{3} \qquad \frac{5}{6} \qquad \frac{4}{5}$$

> The number **above** the line in each fraction gives the number of equal parts which have been taken.
> This number is called the **numerator** of the fraction.

Write in words and figures the fraction of each whole one which is shaded.

7  What is  a  the denominator
          b  the numerator
of each fraction you have written?

8  In the fraction $\frac{3}{8}$
a  what is the 8 called?
   What does it tell you?
b  what is the 3 called?
   What does it tell you?

9  a  Write a fraction with 10 as the denominator and 7 as the numerator.
b  Write this fraction in words.
c  Draw a diagram on squared paper and show this fraction by shading.

10  To find $\frac{7}{8}$ of a number, divide it into ☐ equal parts and take ☐ of the parts.

11  To find $\frac{9}{10}$ of a quantity, divide it into ☐ equal parts and take ☐ of the parts.

# Fractions

**A** The shape represents a **whole one**.

It is divided into strips and squares.

One of the strips is shaded.

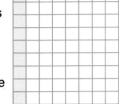

1 How many strips are there?

2 What fraction of the whole is one strip?

3 Into how many small squares is each strip divided?

4 What fraction of one strip is one small square?

5 How many squares are there in the whole?

6 What fraction of the whole is one small square?

---

**£1·00 = 100p**

7 What fraction of £1 is: 1 TEN, 1p?

8 What fraction of 1 TEN is: 3p, 7p?

What fraction of £1 is:

9 3 TENS    10 7 TENS    11 9 TENS

12 1 TWENTY  13 3 TWENTIES  14 80p?

Write in pence the value of:

15 £$\frac{8}{10}$ or £$\frac{4}{5}$    16 $\frac{9}{10}$ of 1 TEN

17 $\frac{2}{5}$ of 1 TWENTY    18 $\frac{1}{10}$ of 1 TWENTY.

---

**1 metre = 100 cm**

19 What fraction of 1 m is: 10 cm, 1 cm?

20 What fraction of 1 m is: 30 cm, 70 cm?

Write in cm the length of:

21 $\frac{7}{100}$ of 1 m    22 $\frac{28}{100}$ of 1 m.

---

**B** Find the value of:

|  | a | b | c |
|---|---|---|---|
| 1 | $\frac{1}{2}$ of 60 | $\frac{1}{4}$ of 60 | $\frac{3}{4}$ of 60 |
| 2 | $\frac{1}{8}$ of 72p | $\frac{3}{8}$ of 72p | $\frac{5}{8}$ of 72p |
| 3 | $\frac{1}{3}$ of 84p | $\frac{1}{6}$ of 84p | $\frac{5}{6}$ of 84p |
| 4 | $\frac{1}{5}$ of £45 | $\frac{3}{5}$ of £45 | $\frac{4}{5}$ of £45 |
| 5 | $\frac{1}{10}$ of 200 g | $\frac{7}{10}$ of 200 g | $\frac{9}{10}$ of 200 g |
| 6 | $\frac{1}{7}$ of 28 ℓ | $\frac{3}{7}$ of 28 ℓ | $\frac{6}{7}$ of 28 ℓ |
| 7 | $\frac{1}{9}$ of 63 m | $\frac{4}{9}$ of 63 m | $\frac{8}{9}$ of 63 m |
| 8 | $\frac{1}{100}$ of 500 g | $\frac{7}{100}$ of 500 g | $\frac{33}{100}$ of 500 g. |

The pie chart gives the expenses of running a shop.

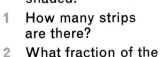

What fraction of the total expenses are

9 light and heat

10 rent    11 wages

12 delivery charges    13 postage?

14 How much is spent on each item if the total expenses are £180?

---

**C**

1 $\frac{5}{6}$ of a number is 45.
 Find   a $\frac{1}{6}$ of the number
    b $\frac{6}{6}$ or all of the number.

2 $\frac{3}{4}$ of a sum of money is 36p.
 Find   a $\frac{1}{4}$ of the sum of the money
    b $\frac{4}{4}$ or all of the money.

3 $\frac{3}{10}$ of a bag of sugar has a mass of 600 g.
 Find   a $\frac{1}{10}$ of the quantity in g
    b the mass of all the sugar in kg.

4 $\frac{7}{8}$ of a length of wood is $73\frac{1}{2}$ cm.
 Find   a $\frac{1}{8}$ of the length
    b the whole of the length in cm.

Find the whole number, sum of money or quantity when:

5 $\frac{2}{3}$ is 50 ℓ    6 $\frac{5}{6}$ is 30 kg

7 $\frac{7}{20}$ is 140    8 $\frac{4}{7}$ is 28p

9 $\frac{3}{5}$ is £63    10 $\frac{7}{100}$ is 21p

11 $\frac{5}{9}$ is 200 g    12 $\frac{7}{8}$ is $3\frac{1}{2}$ km.

13 A man travels 38 km, which is $\frac{2}{7}$ of his journey, by car and the rest by train. Find the total distance of the journey.

14 Susan has $\frac{1}{5}$ of a sum of money and Philip has $\frac{3}{10}$. Together they have 60p. Find the total sum of money.

# Shapes which balance

**A**

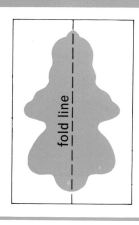

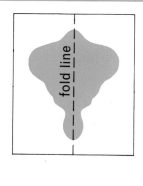

1. Fold a sheet of paper in half.
2. Open it and mark the fold line.
3. Make blots of ink or paint on the fold line on the inside of the paper.
4. Quickly refold the paper and press it firmly.
5. Open the paper again and look at the pattern you have made. Notice that it is the same on each side of the fold line. The shape balances about the fold line.
6. Make more patterns in this way, and check that each balances about the fold line.

**B**

1. Fold a sheet of paper in half by a vertical fold line.
2. On one half of the paper draw a shape which fits along the fold line as in drawing **X**.
3. Cut out this shape through both thicknesses of the paper.
4. Now open the paper and look at the shape. One half of the shape is the same size and looks the same as the other. The whole shape balances about the fold line.

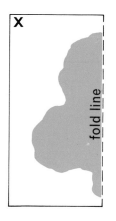

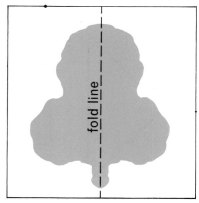

**C**

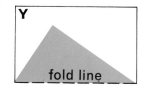

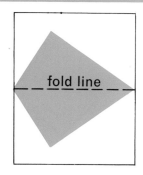

1. Fold a sheet of paper in half by a horizontal fold line.
2. On one half of the paper draw a shape which fits along the fold line as in drawing **Y**.
3. Cut out the shape through both thicknesses of the paper.
4. Open the paper and look at the shape. Does the whole shape balance about the fold line?

5. In the same way, by folding and cutting, make shapes like these.

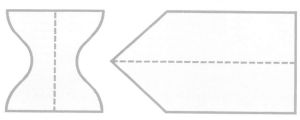

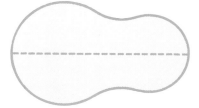

# Shapes which balance   symmetry

The fold line about which a shape balances has a special name.
It is called a **line of symmetry**.
Shapes which balance are called **symmetrical shapes**.

**A**

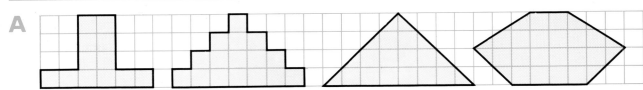

1   The shapes above are symmetrical. Each has one line of symmetry which is vertical.
   Copy the shapes on squared paper and draw the line of symmetry in each.

2   Each of these shapes below has one line of symmetry which is horizontal.
   Copy the shapes on squared paper and draw the line of symmetry in each.

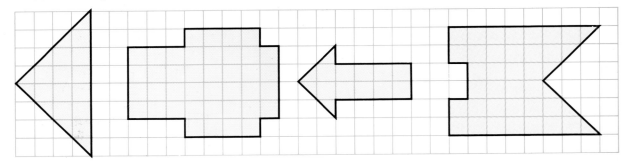

3   Each of the shapes below has a line of symmetry which is oblique.
   Copy the shapes on squared paper and draw a line of symmetry in each.

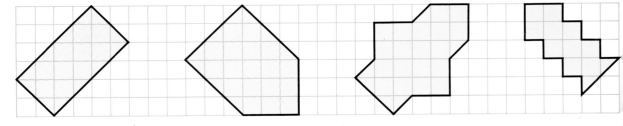

**B**   These are half-shapes. A line of symmetry is shown in each by a dotted line.
   On squared paper draw each complete symmetrical shape.

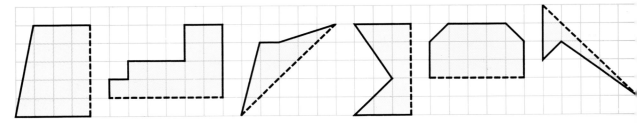

# Shapes which balance   symmetry

**A**  Some shapes have more than one line of symmetry.

1  Copy these shapes on squared paper. To make your drawings larger use cm squared paper. Cut out the shapes you have drawn and letter them **V, W, X, Y, Z**.

2  Find, by folding, the shapes which are not symmetrical.

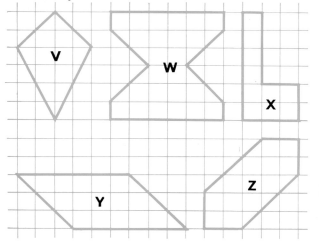

Look at the shapes below. Write the letters of the shapes which have

3  no line of symmetry
4  one line of symmetry
5  two lines of symmetry
6  more than two lines of symmetry.

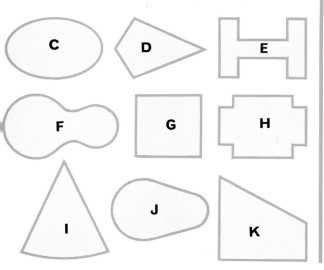

**B**  The shapes of many leaves, plants, insects and birds are symmetrical.

1  Collect six leaves of different shapes. Press them flat on a sheet of paper. Draw round the edge of each leaf and then mark the line of symmetry.

2  Where is the line of symmetry on
   a  the bird       b   the butterfly?

3  Many symmetrical shapes can be seen on buildings. Make a collection of pictures and drawings like these examples.

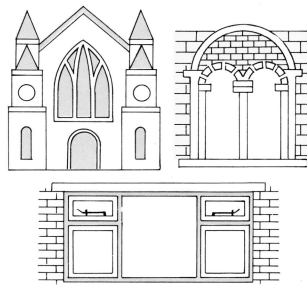

4  Which of the following are symmetrical?
   a bucket      a teaspoon      a dinner-knife
   a 1p coin      a tennis-racket
   a hockey-stick       your partner's face

5  Which are not symmetrical?

# Multiplication and division

**A** Write the answers only.

1. $(8 \times 3) \div 6$
2. $(4 \times 9) \div 3$
3. $(7 \times 0) \div 5$
4. $(6 \times 7) \div 2$
5. $(1 \times 8) \div 4$
6. $(64 \div 8) \times 3$
7. $(81 \div 9) \times 7$
8. $(48 \div 6) \times 5$
9. $(45 \div 5) \times 6$
10. $(32 \div 4) \times 9$

Find the missing number.

11. $45 = 9 \times \square$
12. $8 \times \square = 40$
13. $\square \times 7 = 7$
14. $63 \div \square = 7$
15. $\square \div 5 = 6$
16. $42 \div \square = 6$
17. $9 \times \square = 54$
18. $\square \div 7 = 5$
19. $64 = \square \times 8$
20. $9 \div \square = 1$

Find the value of $x$ in each of these.

21. $45 \div x = 9$
22. $x \times 8 = 48$
23. $4 \times x = 36$
24. $x \div 7 = 3$
25. $\frac{72}{x} = 9$
26. $(4 \times x) = (36 \div 9)$
27. $2 \times 2 \times x = 0$
28. $2x + x = 27$
29. $(42 \div 7) = (x \times 3)$
30. $x + (x + 6) = 20$

Find the missing sign $+$, $-$, $\times$ or $\div$ in place of ●.

31. $2 ● 8 = 4 ● 4$
32. $18 ● 3 = 1 ● 6$
33. $7 ● 8 = 5 ● 3$
34. $24 ● 6 = 10 ● 6$
35. $36 ● 4 = 3 ● 3$
36. $5 ● 5 = 10 ● 15$
37. $4 ● 6 = 3 ● 8$
38. $9 + 9 ● 9 = 3 ● 9$
39. $3 ● 4 = 28 ● 4$
40. $7 ● 2 = 35 ● 7$

**B** Write the answers only.

1. $63 \times 5$
2. $50 \times 6$
3. $74 \times 9$
4. $65 \times 8$
5. $96 \div 3$
6. $140 \div 5$
7. $272 \div 4$
8. $306 \div 6$
9. $525 \div 7$
10. $702 \div 9$
11. $684 \div 6$
12. $912 \div 8$

Check answers **1** to **4** by division and answers **5** to **12** by multiplication.

Write the answers only to the following.

13. $37p \times 2$
14. $18p \times 5$
15. $12p \times 7$
16. $64p \times 4$
17. $46p \times 6$
18. $28p \times 8$
19. $6 \overline{)\, 84p}$
20. $5 \overline{)\, 95p}$
21. $8 \overline{)\, 96p}$
22. $57p \div 3$
23. $92p \div 4$
24. $91p \div 7$

**C** Write the answers only, when you can.

Find the number of times:

1. £6 can be paid from a total of £54
2. 5 cm of ribbon can be cut from $\frac{1}{2}$ m
3. a bottle holding 200 mℓ can be filled from 2 litres of fruit juice
4. a packet containing 50 g can be made from 300 g.

5. Share £6 equally among 8 people. How much does each receive?

6. $1\frac{1}{2}$ kg of sweets are put in equal masses into 10 bags. How many g are there in each bag?

7. David changes 95 pennies for FIVES. How many FIVES does he receive?

8. 136 children in a school are put into 4 equal teams. How many children are there in each team?

9. Find the total of 27, 32, 15, 22.

10. Divide the total by 4 to find the average.

11. Find the average of these prices. 15p, 21p, 17p, 14p, 18p

12. $27 \times 4 = 108$   Write: $108 \div 4 = \square$.

13. $126 \div 7 = 18$   Write: $18 \times 7 = \square$.

Find the missing numbers.

14. $\square \times 6 = 162$
15. $\square \times 8 = 312$
16. $\square \div 9 = 22$
17. $\square \div 7 = 57$

18. When a number is divided by 5, the answer is 47 rem. 3. Find the number.

19. Find the missing numbers.
    a $\square \div 8 = 30$ rem. 7   b $\square \div 9 = 49$ rem. 8

20. Find a $\frac{1}{8}$ of 56p        b $\frac{3}{8}$ of 56p
21. a $\frac{1}{6}$ of 72p        b $\frac{5}{6}$ of 72p
22. a $\frac{1}{10}$ of 40p        b $\frac{7}{10}$ of 40p.

Find the whole when

23. $\frac{1}{6}$ is 13p
24. $\frac{1}{8}$ is 70 cm
25. $\frac{1}{5}$ is £39
26. $\frac{1}{10}$ is 55 g.

# Money £s and pence

## A

£5·37 is 5 pounds 37 pence.

1 Write these sums of money as £s and pence.
   a £2·60   b £3·07   c £0·28

2 Write these sums of money using the £ sign. Remember to omit the 'p'.
   a 69p   b 13p   c 4p

3 Write as £s.
   a 392p   b 270p   c 403p

$$£2·46 = \begin{array}{l} £2 \text{ and } 46 \text{ pence} \\ £2, 4 \text{ TENS}, 6 \text{ pence} \\ 24 \text{ TENS and } 6 \text{ pence} \\ 246 \text{ pence} \end{array}$$

Look at the example above and then write and complete:

4 £3·12 = £□ and □ pence
   = £□, □ TEN, □ pence
   = □ TENS and □ pence
   = □ pence

5 Write these sums of money in the same four different ways.
   a £5·90      b £4·05

Write and complete each of the following.

6 £2·35 = £□, □ TENS, □ p

7 £8·50 = £□, □ TENS, □ p

8 £3·62 = □ TENS, □ p

9 203p = £□, □ TENS, □ p

10 £0·85 = £□, □ TENS, □ p

11 470p = □ TENS, □ p

12 £5·03 = £□, □ TENS, □ p

13 £0·07 = □ TENS, □ p

What is the value of the 5 in each of these sums of money?

14 £15·20   15 £52·20   16 £0·35

17 £0·05   18 £7·54   19 £510·26

Arrange these amounts in order, the largest first.

20 £0·95, £1·05, £1·55, £1·50

21 £2·02, £2·22, £2·00, £2·20

## B

When making up sums of money to pay bills or for purchases, it is convenient to give the least number of notes and coins.
Look at the example.

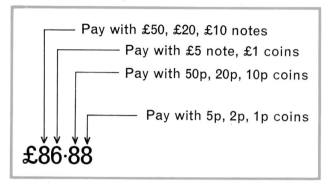

Pay with £50, £20, £10 notes
Pay with £5 note, £1 coins
Pay with 50p, 20p, 10p coins
Pay with 5p, 2p, 1p coins

£86·88

Draw the table below.
Make up the sums of money by using the least number of notes and coins.

|   |        | notes | | coins | | | | | | | |
|---|--------|-------|-----|-----|-----|-----|-----|-----|-----|-----|
|   |        | £10   | £5  | £1  | 50p | 20p | 10p | 5p  | 2p  | 1p  |
| 1 | £8·76  |       | 1   | 3   | 1   | 1   |     | 1   |     | 1   |
| 2 | £2·42  |       |     |     |     |     |     |     |     |     |
| 3 | £13·77 |       |     |     |     |     |     |     |     |     |
| 4 | £6·55  |       |     |     |     |     |     |     |     |     |
| 5 | £0·98  |       |     |     |     |     |     |     |     |     |
| 6 | £9·63  |       |     |     |     |     |     |     |     |     |
| 7 | £16·80 |       |     |     |     |     |     |     |     |     |

When shopping, always check the change.
In which of these examples is there a mistake in the change? Find the error in each case.

|    | money given | amount spent | change given |
|----|-------------|--------------|--------------|
| 8  | 1 FIFTY     | 41p          | 2 TWOS, 1 FIVE |
| 9  | 4 TWENTIES  | 73p          | 1 FIVE, 1p |
| 10 | £1          | 25p          | 3 TWENTIES, 1 FIVE |
| 11 | £1          | 64p          | 1 TEN, 3 FIVES, 1p |
| 12 | £5 note     | 95p          | 3 × £1, 1 FIVE |
| 13 | £5 note     | £2·05        | 2 × £1, 1 FIFTY, 5 FIVES |

# Money £s and pence

**A** Write the answers as £s.
Remember to omit the 'p' from the answers.

| 1 | 55p 11p +23p | 2 | 36p 59p +14p | 3 | 28p 82p +19p | 4 | 55p 75p +10p | 5 | 9p 44p +58p |
|---|---|---|---|---|---|---|---|---|---|

| 6 | 37p 73p +85p | 7 | 56p 87p +97p | 8 | 49p 7p +25p | 9 | 4p 12p +30p | 10 | 16p 73p +61p |
|---|---|---|---|---|---|---|---|---|---|

Write these sums of money in columns and find the total of each.

11 43p, £2·02, £1·34    12 £1·32, 58p, £3·05    13 £0·85, 96p, £6·37

14 £2·51, £1·07, 35p    15 £2·41, £3·72, £4·86    16 £5·87, £3·45, 78p

Write the answers only.

17 29p × 6    18 39p × 4    19 70p × 5    20 14p × 8    21 19p × 9

22 17p × 7    23 68p × 3    24 45p × 10    25 87p × 2    26 48p × 5

**B** Write the answers only.
Remember to put the 0 after the £ sign when there are no £s in the answer.

| 1 | £ 1·96 −1·52 | 2 | £ 1·48 −0·72 | 3 | £ 1·20 −0·86 | 4 | £ 1·08 −0·33 | 5 | £ 1·23 −0·47 |
|---|---|---|---|---|---|---|---|---|---|

| 6 | £ 2·94 −2·58 | 7 | £ 3·17 −2·82 | 8 | £ 5·30 −4·73 | 9 | £ 4·00 −3·49 | 10 | £ 2·16 −1·38 |
|---|---|---|---|---|---|---|---|---|---|

Write these sums of money in columns and find the difference between:

11 £2·76 and 32p    12 £2·07 and £3·09    13 87p and £2·14

14 £3·95 and £0·75    15 £1·38 and £5·24    16 £5·00 and 98p.

Write the answers only.

17 3) £1·68    18 5) £1·85    19 4) £2·96    20 7) £3·29    21 6) £2·76

22 £1·96 ÷ 2    23 £1·88 ÷ 4    24 £3·52 ÷ 8    25 £1·70 ÷ 5    26 £2·25 ÷ 9

**C**

1 Mother spent £1·27, 96p and 84p.
  a How much did she spend altogether?
  b Find the change from £3 and a FIFTY.

2 3 kg of meat costs £5·04.
How much is ½ kg?

3 By how much is three times £1·06 greater than four times 65p?

4 A boy is paid £1·35 per week for delivering newspapers.
How much does he receive for 4 weeks?

5 5 metres of cloth cost £2·85.
Find the cost of
  a 1 metre    b 3 metres    c 7 metres

6 Joan has £6 which is 8 times as much as David has. How much has David?

# Time   12-hour clock

**A** Write these times in figures using a.m. or p.m.

1 quarter past six in the morning
2 four forty-five in the afternoon
3 quarter to eleven at night
4 five and twenty to ten in the morning
5 seven twenty-five in the evening
6 nine minutes to midnight
7 thirteen minutes to noon
8 Write in figures and then in words the time shown on each clock face.

morning times

afternoon or evening times

Write in figures the correct time if:
9 clock **a** is 5 minutes slow
10 clock **b** is 10 minutes fast
11 clock **c** is 8 minutes slow
12 clock **d** is 9 minutes fast
13 clock **e** is 20 minutes slow
14 clock **f** is a quarter of an hour fast.

15 Write in words the time shown on each 12-hour digital clock.

16 Write in figures the times half an hour earlier of clocks **g**, **h** and **i**, and the times half an hour later of clocks **j**, **k** and **l**.

**B** Find the number of minutes to the next hour from:
1 9.46    2 1.03    3 11.18    4 6.39.

How many minutes are there from:
5 1.15 a.m. to 2.15 a.m.
6 3.40 p.m. to 4.10 p.m.
7 11.50 a.m. to 12.30 p.m.
8 2.46 p.m. to 3.07 p.m.
9 9.51 p.m. to 10.12 p.m.
10 11.34 p.m. to 12.24 a.m?

Find the number of hours and minutes from the given a.m. times to noon and the p.m. times to midnight.
11 10.40 a.m.    12 6.18 a.m.    13 8.25 a.m.
14 7.35 p.m.    15 9.30 p.m.    16 5.08 p.m.

Find the number of hours and minutes from noon to
17 1.50 p.m.    18 3.47 p.m.    19 8.04 p.m.
and from midnight to
20 2.35 a.m.    21 6.53 a.m.    22 10.12 a.m.

How many hours and minutes from:
23 11.30 a.m. to 2.00 p.m.
24 10.45 a.m. to 1.30 p.m.
25 9.10 p.m. to 12.50 a.m.
26 11.53 p.m. to 1.46 a.m.
27 7.30 a.m. to 4.15 p.m.
28 10.25 a.m. to 2.30 p.m?

**C** **Minutes and seconds**

Very short periods of time are measured in seconds, often with a stop-watch.

Find in seconds the time taken
1 to write your name and address
2 to change your shoes
3 to read five lines from a story-book.

Which of the four given times do you think right for each of the following activities?
4 counting to 50: 5 min, 2 min, 40 s, 10 s
5 running 50 m: 10 s, 5 min, 1 min, 30 s

# Time and the calendar

## A

**Facts to remember**

60 seconds (s)=1 minute
60 minutes (min)=1 hour
24 hours (h)=1 day
7 days=1 week
52 weeks=1 year
365 days=1 year

**Days in the months**

April, June, September, November — 30 days

January, March, May, July, August, October, December — 31 days

February — 28 days
(Leap year every 4th year — 29 days)

Place a strip of paper alongside the columns of examples.

Write the answers only.

Work quickly and try to beat the clock: 7 min for the 20 answers.

Write the number of:

1  seconds in $\frac{1}{2}$ min
2  seconds in $\frac{3}{4}$ min
3  seconds in $1\frac{1}{4}$ min
4  min in $\frac{1}{4}$ h
5  min in $1\frac{3}{4}$ h
6  min in $\frac{1}{6}$ h
7  min in $\frac{1}{10}$ h
8  min in $\frac{1}{12}$ h
9  min in $\frac{2}{3}$ h
10  min in 5 h
11  h in 1 day
12  days in 6 weeks
13  days in a leap year
14  days in July
15  days in April
16  days in August
17  days in May
18  days in November
19  days in March
20  weeks in a year.

Mark the answers and correct any mistakes in full.

## B

1  Monday is the first day of the week. Name
   a  the third day
   b  the sixth day of the week.

2  1st May is on Sunday. Write the dates of all the Tuesdays in that month.

3  John began a ten-day holiday on Wednesday, 28th September. Give the day and the date on which he returned.

4  Name these months of the year.
   a  the 4th month    b  the 6th month
   c  the 9th month    d  the 11th month

A leap year comes every four years. If the last two numbers of the year are divisible by 4, the year is a leap year.

5  Which of these years were leap years?
   1728,  1804,  1894,  1936,  1978

6  Julia's date of birth is 15.7.76.
   a  In which month was she born?
   b  How old will she be on her birthday in 1985?

7  In which year will Julia be
   a  21 years old    b  50 years old?

8  Write in figures your own date of birth and that of each of four friends.

9
| name | date of birth |
|---|---|
| Alan | 24. 11. 72 |
| Jill | 13. 9. 65 |
| Mr. Brown | 16. 4. 48 |

a  In which month was each person born?
b  Find the age in years of each person on the 31st December 2000.

10  We live in the 20th century. Guy Fawkes was born in 1570 and died in 1606.
   a  In which century was he born?
   b  In which century did he die?

When reckoning periods of time in days, **the first day is not counted** unless you are told that the dates are **inclusive**.

How many days are there from:

11  5th May to 21st May
12  27th June to 8th July
13  14th Aug. to 5th Sept.
14  29th Oct. to 3rd Dec?

How many days inclusive from:

15  Sat. 4th May to Sat. 11th May
16  2nd Feb. to 1st March 1982?

# Charts and graphs

**A** Paul and Susan made a count of the traffic which passed along a busy road near the school.
They counted the number of motor cycles, motor cars, buses and trucks which went by in a quarter of an hour.
They then made this chart by drawing one picture to represent one vehicle.

| **First count** | motor cycles | ⊤ ⊤ ⊤ ⊤ ⊤ ⊤ ⊤ ⊤ |
|---|---|---|
| | motor cars | 🚗🚗🚗🚗🚗🚗🚗🚗🚗🚗🚗🚗🚗🚗🚗🚗🚗🚗🚗🚗🚗🚗🚗🚗 |
| | buses | 🚌🚌🚌🚌🚌🚌🚌 |
| | trucks and vans | 🚚🚚🚚🚚🚚🚚🚚🚚🚚🚚🚚🚚🚚🚚 |

1 Find the number of   a  motor cycles
  b  trucks and vans which passed.

2 By how many was the number of buses less than the number of motor cars?

3 How many more trucks and vans than buses passed by?

4 a  How many of each kind of vehicle?
  b  How many altogether?

5 If one picture represents
  a  2 vehicles     b  5 vehicles,
  what is the number of each kind?

6 Susan counted 36 pedestrians who passed by. Make a drawing to show this number. Let 🚶 represent 3 pedestrians.

7 If 🚶 represented 4 pedestrians, how many pictures would Susan draw?

**B** At the same time next day, Paul and Susan made a second traffic count, and then drew a graph to show the number of each kind of vehicle.

Instead of drawing pictures, one square on 5 mm graph paper was used to represent one vehicle.

**Second count**

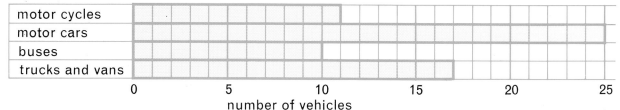

number of vehicles

1 What does one square represent on the horizontal axis?

2 What is shown on the vertical axis?

3 Make a list of the kinds of vehicles and find the number of each.

4 What is the total number of vehicles?

5 If each square represented
  a  4 vehicles     b  10 vehicles,
  what would be the number of each kind of vehicle in each case?

6 Draw a graph to show:
24 motor cycles
32 cars
14 buses
18 trucks and vans
56 pedestrians.

On the vertical axis show the kinds of vehicles and the pedestrians.
On the horizontal axis mark the scale:
  2 vehicles or 2 pedestrians to 1 square.

# Graphs

**A** Paul and Susan made two more traffic counts at the same time on the next two days.

A record sheet was made for each count and a mark (/) for each vehicle which passed was shown on the correct row.

These are the record sheets.

**Third count**

| kinds of vehicle | number | total |
|---|---|---|
| motor cycles | JHT JHT JHT JHT I | |
| motor cars | JHT JHT JHT JHT JHT III | |
| buses | JHT JHT JHT | |
| trucks and vans | JHT JHT JHT III | |

**Fourth count**

| kinds of vehicle | number | total |
|---|---|---|
| motor cycles | JHT | |
| motor cars | JHT JHT JHT JHT JHT JHT JHT IIII | |
| buses | JHT III | |
| trucks and vans | JHT JHT JHT JHT I | |

1 From the record sheets, find the total number of vehicles of each kind for
  a the third count    b the fourth count.
2 Check the totals from the answer book.
3 On 5 mm squared paper draw two graphs to show these numbers. On the vertical axis write the kinds of vehicles.
  On the horizontal axis mark the scale:
    1 division to represent 1 vehicle.

From the graph of the third count, answer the following.

4 Write the kinds of vehicle in order, putting the largest number of vehicles first.
5 What is the difference between the greatest and smallest number of vehicles?
6 Find the total number of vehicles in the count.
7 Answer questions **4**, **5** and **6** from the graph of the fourth count.

**B**

| kinds of vehicle | 1st count | 2nd count | 3rd count | 4th count | X |
|---|---|---|---|---|---|
| motor cycles | | | | | |
| motor cars | | | | | |
| buses | | | | | |
| trucks and vans | | | | | |
| Y | | | | | grand total |

1 Draw the table and write in the correct places the numbers which Paul and Susan obtained from each of the four counts.
2 Now find and enter in the table
  a the total number of each kind of vehicle for the four counts (column **X**)
  b the total number of vehicles in each count (row **Y**).
3 Check the table when completed by finding the **grand total**.
  The total of column **X** should be the same as the total of row **Y**.

4 On 5 mm squared paper draw a graph to show the total of each kind of vehicle.
  On the horizontal axis mark the scale:
    1 division to represent 5 vehicles.
5 Write the kinds of vehicle in order, putting the largest number of vehicles first.
6 Make a record sheet and then make similar counts of the traffic which passes your school. First, get your teacher's permission and make sure you take up a **safe position**.
  Draw graphs to show the counts.

# Number thousands, hundreds, tens and units

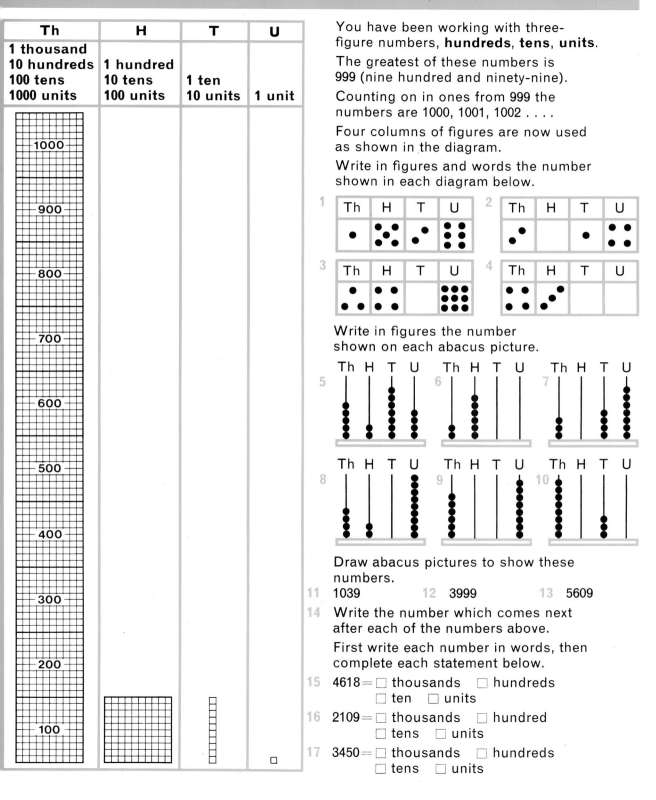

| Th | H | T | U |
|---|---|---|---|
| 1 thousand<br>10 hundreds<br>100 tens<br>1000 units | 1 hundred<br>10 tens<br>100 units | 1 ten<br>10 units | 1 unit |

You have been working with three-figure numbers, **hundreds**, **tens**, **units**.

The greatest of these numbers is 999 (nine hundred and ninety-nine).

Counting on in ones from 999 the numbers are 1000, 1001, 1002 . . . .

Four columns of figures are now used as shown in the diagram.

Write in figures and words the number shown in each diagram below.

Write in figures the number shown on each abacus picture.

Draw abacus pictures to show these numbers.

11  1039          12  3999          13  5609

14  Write the number which comes next after each of the numbers above.

First write each number in words, then complete each statement below.

15  4618 = ☐ thousands  ☐ hundreds
            ☐ ten  ☐ units

16  2109 = ☐ thousands  ☐ hundred
            ☐ tens  ☐ units

17  3450 = ☐ thousands  ☐ hundreds
            ☐ tens  ☐ units

# **Number** thousands, hundreds, tens and units

## A

Draw the columns and write in the numbers putting the figures in the correct places.
The first is done for you.

1 two thousand four hundred and thirty-six

| Th | H | T | U |
|----|---|---|---|
| 2  | 4 | 3 | 6 |
|    |   |   |   |

2 three thousand and seven
3 one thousand and eighty
4 five thousand six hundred
5 six thousand and thirteen
6 eight thousand
7 four thousand and fifty-six
8 nine thousand and ten

### Counting exercises

Count aloud with a partner in turn:

9 in **thousands** from 1000 to 9000
10 in **hundreds** from a 800 to 1200
                   b 3900 to 4300
11 in **tens** from a 980 to 1020
                   b 2990 to 3020
12 in **ones** from a 996 to 1005
                   b 2009 to 2016.

Write in figures the number which is:

13 1 more than    a 4069   b 1999
                  c 3209   d 4599
14 10 more than   a 993    b 1094
                  c 2006   d 3705
15 100 more than  a 1507   b 2031
                  c 5000   d 3947
16 1 less than     a 1010   b 2800
                  c 1750   d 3000
17 10 less than   a 1837   b 1014
                  c 3200   d 2006
18 100 less than  a 4000   b 2709
                  c 1946   d 3030.

Write the answers only.

19 804 + 200
20 1316 + 500
21 1830 + 70
22 1109 + 900
23 2352 + 50
24 3098 + 400
25 2000 − 900
26 1704 − 600
27 1988 − 30
28 2100 − 500
29 1703 − 80
30 3007 − 700

## B

1

Write:
a the value of the 6
b the value of the 4
c the value of the 8
d the value of the 5.

In each of these numbers write the value of the figure underlined.

2 315
3 1097
4 4716
5 2854
6 6001
7 3107

8 Arrange 3, 8, 1, 6 to make
a the greatest
b the least possible number.

9 Arrange these figures to make the greatest possible numbers.
a 7, 0, 3, 9    b 4, 8, 7, 0

10 Write and fill in the missing numbers.

3659
□ thousands □ hundreds □ units
□ hundreds □ tens □ units
□ tens □ units
□ hundreds □ units
□ thousands □ units

Write these numbers as:

11 thousands and units      a 2008  b 4904
12 hundreds and units       a 1074  b 2506
13 tens and units             a 3037  b 5108
14 hundreds, tens, units    a 4082  b 7205
15 thousands, hundreds, units                 a 6130  b 9056

16       $x$   $y$
**7777**   How many times greater is the 7 at $x$ than the 7 at $y$?

17       $y$   $x$
**4444**   How many times smaller is the 4 at $x$ than the 4 at $y$?

How many times is:

18 2030 greater than 203
19 4600 greater than 46
20 307 smaller than 3070
21 19 smaller than 1900?

Write the answers only to the following.

22 92 × 100
23 347 × 10
24 4500 ÷ 100
25 7230 ÷ 10

# Lines and angles

**A** The drawing shows the end wall of a class-room.

Each line or edge is marked by a letter.

Find the lines or edges which are:

1 parallel to the floor
2 parallel to the sides of the room
3 perpendicular to the floor
4 perpendicular to the top edge of the blackboard.

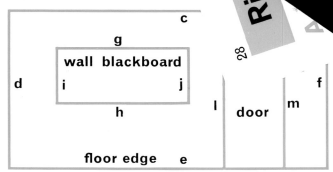

5 Draw two parallel lines which are
  a horizontal and 15 mm apart
  b vertical and 23 mm apart
  c oblique and 18 mm apart.

6 Draw  a a horizontal line
        b a vertical line   c an oblique line.
7 Use a set square to draw two lines perpendicular to each.

---

**B**

> **Remember** An acute angle is less than a right angle.
> An obtuse angle is greater than a right angle but less than two right angles.

Name, by the letters, the angles which are:

1 right angles   2 acute angles   3 obtuse angles. Use a set square if you wish.

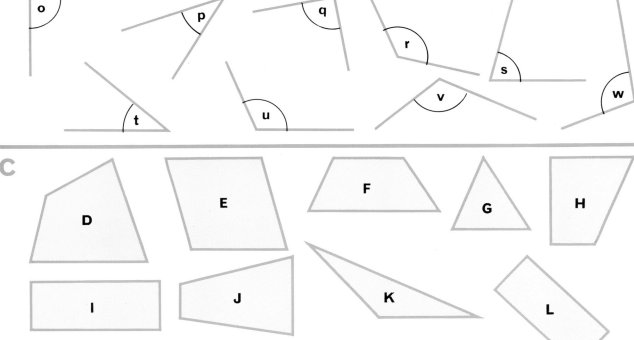

**C**

Write the letters of the shapes in which there are:

1 sides perpendicular to the base
2 two pairs of parallel sides
3 one pair of parallel sides

4 three acute angles
5 two obtuse angles
6 two or more right angles.

# ...ht angles  degrees

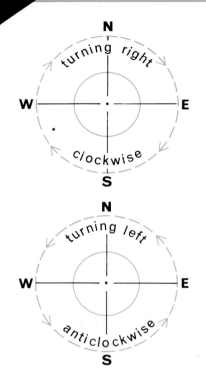

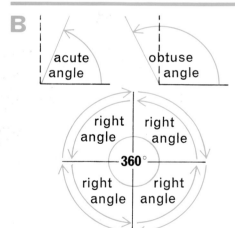

The right angle is used as a unit to measure **turns** or **rotations**.

1  A girl faces north. She turns completely round once.
   a  In which direction is she then facing?
   b  Through how many right angles has she turned?

2  If she made  a  2 complete turns     b  5 complete turns, through how many right angles has she turned?

3  Through how many right angles does she turn if she makes
   a  a half turn to face in the opposite direction
   b  a quarter turn     c  a three-quarter turn?

Look at the diagrams which show that turns are made clockwise (to the right) or anticlockwise (to the left).

4  John faces east. To face north, through how many right angles does he turn
   a  clockwise     b  anticlockwise?

5  Mary faces west. To face south, through how many right angles does she turn
   a  clockwise     b  anticlockwise?

6  Peter faces south. He turns clockwise through three right angles. In which direction is he now facing?

## B

acute angle

obtuse angle

right angle | right angle
—360°—
right angle | right angle

A smaller unit than a right angle is required to measure **acute** and **obtuse angles**, as the diagram shows.

Many centuries ago, the people of Babylon divided a complete turn into 360 equal parts or **degrees (360°)**.

This unit for measuring angles is still used today.

1  How many degrees are there in a right angle?

2  Write and complete:
   1 complete turn = ☐ right angles = ☐ degrees = ☐°
   $\frac{1}{2}$ complete turn = ☐ right angles = ☐ degrees = ☐°
   $\frac{1}{4}$ complete turn = ☐ right angles = ☐ degrees = ☐°
   $\frac{3}{4}$ complete turn = ☐ right angles = ☐ degrees = ☐°

## C

How many degrees are there in:

1  $\frac{1}{2}$ right angle        2  $\frac{1}{4}$ right angle

3  $\frac{1}{3}$ right angle        4  $\frac{1}{6}$ right angle

5  the angle at the centre of a circle?

6  How many hours does it take the hour-hand of a clock to turn through
   a  360°     b  180°     c  270°?

7  How many minutes does it take the minute-hand of a clock to pass through:
   a  360°     b  90°     c  60°
   d  180°     e  30°     f  45°?

8  How many
   a  right angles
   b  degrees
   are there in a straight angle?

a straight angle

# Angles  45°, 60°, 30°, set squares

**A**

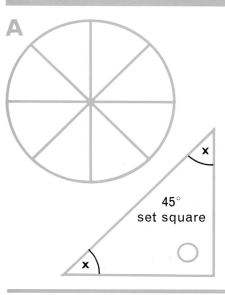

45° set square

1  On a piece of stiff paper draw a large circle. Cut it out.
2  Fold the circle into eight equal parts.
3  Open the circle and using a ruler, draw along the crease marks.
4  The circle now looks like that in the diagram.
   How many equal angles are there at the centre?
5  What fraction is one of these equal angles of
   a  one right angle or 90°     b  360°?
6  How many degrees in each of these angles?
7  Cut out each of these angles. Fit them one on the other and check that they are all 45°.
8  Get a 45° set square. Fit one of the 45° angles into each angle marked **x** in the set square.
   It should fit exactly.
9  Which angles can be drawn using a 45° set square?

**B**

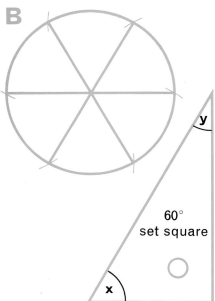

60° set square

1  Draw another large circle on a piece of stiff paper.
2  Mark off the **radius** round the **circumference**.
3  There are six points. Join them with lines passing through the centre (**diameters**).
4  How many equal angles are there at the centre of the circle?
5  Cut out the circle and then each of the angles.
   Fit them on top of each other and see if they are all the same size.
6  What fraction of the angle at the centre (360°) is one of these angles? What does it measure in degrees?
7  Take one of these angles and fold it exactly into two equal parts.
   How many degrees are there in the angle of each part?
8  Get a set square like that shown in the diagram.
   Which of your angles fit the angles marked **x** and **y**?
9  Which angles can be drawn using a 60° set square?

**C**  Angles of 90°, 45°, 60° and 30° can be drawn using the set squares.
By fitting these angles together, draw angles of:
1  75°      2  120°
3  105°      4  135°
5  150°.
The first example is done for you.

Find in degrees the size of each of the equal angles marked at the centre of these circles.

6    7     8

# Angles   compass directions

**A**   The compass is an instrument used to find direction.

The pointer of the compass always shows the **north** direction and this compass card gives eight points of the compass.

Get a compass, examine it and find out how it works.

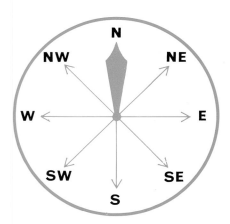

1   Make a compass card.
   a   On a piece of stiff paper draw and cut out a large circle.
   b   Fold the circle into eight equal parts and mark the crease lines in pencil.
   c   Write the eight directions as shown in the diagram.

2   What do these abbreviations stand for?
   NE    SE    SW    NW

3   What is the size, in degrees, of each angle at the centre?

4   A boy faces N. He turns clockwise to face SE. Through how many degrees has he turned?

5   From N, through how many degrees does he turn clockwise to face:
   a   S    b   W    c   SW    d   NW?

6   An aeroplane is flying N. Through how many degrees does it turn to fly NE?

Turning clockwise, how many degrees from:

7   E to SE
8   SW to W
9   SE to S
10   SW to NW
11   E to SW

12   W to NE
13   SE to NW
14   NW to NE
15   S to NW
16   SE to SW?

**B**

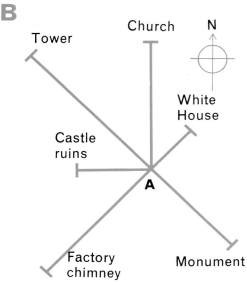

A boy scout stands at the top of a hill marked **A**. In which direction is he looking when he faces:

1   the Monument
2   the church
3   the tower
4   the Castle ruins
5   the factory chimney
6   the White House?

Through how many degrees clockwise does he turn from facing:

7   the tower to face the White House
8   the factory chimney to face the church
9   the Castle ruins to face the Monument
10   the church to face the tower?

The map is drawn to a scale of 2 cm to 1 km, that is 2 cm represent 1 km.

11   Find the actual distance in km from the hill top **A** to each of the places marked on the map.

12   Get an Ordnance Survey map of the district in which you live.

Find your city, town or village and name at least two places which are approximately:
   a   N    b   S    c   NE    d   SW    of your city, town or village.

# Addition graded practice

First work section **A**. Mark the answers and correct any mistakes.
Then work and correct section **B**.
Do the same with Sections **C**, **D** and **E**. Write the answers only.

**First add upwards then check by adding downwards**.

**A**

| 1 | 304 | 2 | 5 | 3 | 237 | 4 | 81 | 5 | 202 |
|---|---|---|---|---|---|---|---|---|---|
| | 21 | | 31 | | 502 | | 404 | | 634 |
| | +452 | | +540 | | +340 | | +503 | | +212 |

**B**

| 1 | 16 | 2 | 34 | 3 | 2040 | 4 | 305 | 5 | 1404 |
|---|---|---|---|---|---|---|---|---|---|
| | 302 | | 214 | | 203 | | 2212 | | 2062 |
| | +1452 | | +1022 | | + 447 | | + 463 | | +1338 |

**C**

| 1 | £ | 2 | £ | 3 | £ | 4 | £ | 5 | £ |
|---|---|---|---|---|---|---|---|---|---|
| | 4·14 | | 6·27 | | 21·46 | | 34·04 | | 0·19 |
| | 0·03 | | 0·32 | | 3·07 | | 0·29 | | 53·08 |
| | 2·09 | | 5·04 | | 10·14 | | 1·37 | | 1·65 |
| | +0·50 | | +0·03 | | + 2·00 | | +23·16 | | +32·02 |

**D**

| 1 | 26 | 2 | 149 | 3 | 475 | 4 | 2098 | 5 | 764 |
|---|---|---|---|---|---|---|---|---|---|
| | 7 | | 256 | | 1208 | | 1567 | | 3305 |
| | 34 | | 33 | | 763 | | 304 | | 86 |
| | +252 | | +362 | | + 94 | | +1782 | | +1437 |

**E**

| 1 | £ | 2 | £ | 3 | £ | 4 | £ | 5 | £ |
|---|---|---|---|---|---|---|---|---|---|
| | 7·39 | | 39·01 | | 13·73 | | 24·65 | | 8·40 |
| | 20·05 | | 8·00 | | 38·95 | | 8·34 | | 37·29 |
| | 13·20 | | 21·43 | | 10·17 | | 17·07 | | 0·86 |
| | + 0·24 | | + 0·52 | | + 9·41 | | + 9·94 | | +21·08 |

**F**

1 Write these sums of money in columns and then find the total.
£29·06,    85p,    £17·84,    £0·92

2 Write the answers only. First add from right to left and check by adding from left to right.
a  847+63+196+7
b  2058+695+107+1471

3 The masses of three parcels are 370 g, 965 g and 850 g.
Find their total mass in grams.
Write the answer in kg and g.

4 The measurements of four pieces of wood are 95 cm, 84 cm, 78 cm and 109 cm.
Find the total length in m and cm.

Look at Mrs Brown's bills for May.

| Shops | Week ending | | | |
|---|---|---|---|---|
| | May 7 | May 14 | May 21 | May 28 |
| Butcher | £3·74 | £4·07 | £2·95 | £4·68 |
| Baker | £1·96 | £1·45 | £0·79 | £1·08 |
| Grocer | £5·42 | £6·50 | £5·84 | £4·98 |
| Greengrocer | £4·13 | £3·23 | £4·36 | £3·28 |

5 Find the total amount she paid during each of the four weeks (four answers).

6 What is the grand total of these amounts?

7 Find the total amount she paid at each shop during the month.

8 What is the grand total of these amounts? Totals **6** and **8** should be the same.

# Subtraction  graded practice

First work Section **A**. Mark the answers and correct any mistakes.

Then work and correct Section **B**.

Do the same with Sections **C** and **D**. Write the answers only.

**Check by adding the answer to the bottom line of the example.**

**The total is the same as the top line of the example.**

**A**

| | | | | | | | | | |
|---|---|---|---|---|---|---|---|---|---|
| 1 | 739<br>−516 | 2 | 586<br>− 70 | 3 | 1487<br>−1384 | 4 | 2739<br>−1402 | 5 | 3075<br>−1023 |
| 6 | £<br>3·68<br>−2·50 | 7 | £<br>8·14<br>−8·02 | 8 | £<br>28·61<br>−10·01 | 9 | £<br>50·77<br>−20·50 | 10 | £<br>40·09<br>−30·06 |

**B**

| | | | | | | | | | |
|---|---|---|---|---|---|---|---|---|---|
| 1 | 340<br>−127 | 2 | 780<br>−314 | 3 | 1470<br>− 266 | 4 | 2904<br>−1832 | 5 | 6500<br>−1465 |
| 6 | £<br>4·80<br>−3·57 | 7 | £<br>8·09<br>−0·53 | 8 | £<br>30·76<br>−23·74 | 9 | £<br>70·95<br>− 5·60 | 10 | £<br>50·00<br>−13·38 |

**C**

| | | | | | | | | | |
|---|---|---|---|---|---|---|---|---|---|
| 1 | 356<br>−167 | 2 | 873<br>− 98 | 3 | 1800<br>−1437 | 4 | 3185<br>− 97 | 5 | 4976<br>−4879 |
| 6 | £<br>2·64<br>−1·37 | 7 | £<br>5·28<br>−3·09 | 8 | £<br>16·82<br>− 5·77 | 9 | £<br>21·36<br>−20·29 | 10 | £<br>31·40<br>−26·65 |

**D**

| | | | | | | | | | |
|---|---|---|---|---|---|---|---|---|---|
| 1 | 800<br>− 57 | 2 | 916<br>−807 | 3 | 1013<br>− 89 | 4 | 3560<br>−2780 | 5 | 5900<br>−4972 |
| 6 | £<br>9·62<br>−3·05 | 7 | £<br>7·08<br>−7·04 | 8 | £<br>21·05<br>− 9·63 | 9 | £<br>33·70<br>−23·92 | 10 | £<br>58·93<br>−48·76 |

**E**

1 Find the difference between:
1 289 and 96    2 920 g and 350 g
3 £2·83 and £5·00    4 58 cm and 1 m 25 cm.

5 Take 947 from 1209.

6 From £10·50 take £0·89.

7 Of the 406 children in a school 59 were absent. How many children were present?

8 The price of a dress costing £13·40 was reduced by 85p. Find the new price.

9 a How many cm are there in 2 m 54 cm?
   b What length in cm is 87 cm less?

10 a How many g are there in 1 kg 700 g?
   b Find a mass in g which is 950 g less.

11 Mother paid two bills, one for £3·68 and the other for £7·43.
   a How much did she pay altogether?
   b How much change from three £5 notes

12 Reduce by one quarter the price of a coat costing £24·96.

# Length   centimetres and millimetres

**A**  **Estimating and measuring to the nearest cm**

c
d                                                        e
f
        g
h

1  Estimate in cm the length of each of the lines **c, d, e, f, g, h**.
2  Then measure them to the nearest cm.
3  Draw this table and keep a record of your estimates
   and measurements. Find the error in each case.
   If the estimate is too long, show the error with a +.
   If the estimate is too short, show the error with a −.
4  Draw with a straight edge, not a ruler,
   several horizontal, vertical and oblique
   lines of different lengths.
5  Estimate and measure each line to the
   nearest cm.
   Find the error and keep a record of your
   work.
   Practise regularly until you can estimate
   short lengths in cm with accuracy.

| line | estimate cm | actual measure cm | error + or − cm |
|------|-------------|-------------------|-----------------|
| c    |             |                   |                 |
| d    |             |                   |                 |
| e    |             |                   |                 |
| f    |             |                   |                 |
| g    |             |                   |                 |
| h    |             |                   |                 |
|      |             |                   |                 |

**B**  Measuring to the nearest cm gives an approximate length.
To get more accurate measurements a smaller unit than the centimetre is needed.
The **centimetre** is therefore divided into **10 equal parts** each of which is called a
**millimetre (mm)**.

| cm | 1 | 2 | 3 | 4 | 5 | 6 | 7 | 8 | 9 | 10 | 11 | 12 | 13 | 14 | 15 |
|----|---|---|---|---|---|---|---|---|---|----|----|----|----|----|----|
| mm | 10 | 20 | 30 | 40 | 50 | 60 | 70 | 80 | 90 | 100 | 110 | 120 | 130 | 140 | 150 |

From this drawing of a piece of a ruler,
find how many mm there are in:

1  a  3 cm          b  9 cm           c  14 cm
2  a  2 cm 7 mm     b  5 cm 2 mm      c  10 cm 5 mm
3  a  $6\frac{1}{2}$ cm        b  12 cm 9 mm     c  15 cm 3 mm.

Write these measurements in cm and mm.

4  a  14 mm         b  18 mm          c  35 mm
5  a  60 mm         b  97 mm          c  113 mm
6  a  102 mm        b  150 mm         c  200 mm

Another way of writing cm and mm is to
**separate them by a point** and write the
answer as cm.

e.g. 27 mm = 2 cm 7 mm = 2.7 cm

In this way, change the following to cm.

7  a  19 mm         b  25 mm          c  50 mm
8  a  73 mm         b  108 mm         c  205 mm
9  Get a ruler marked in cm and mm.
   Write the greatest length shown on it
   a  in cm        b  in mm.

34

# Length   centimetres and millimetres

The drawing shows a piece of a ruler marked in cm and mm.

1 Write the length of each line **x**, **y** and **z**
  a in mm    b in cm and mm    c in cm.

2 a What is the length of each line to the nearest cm?
  b By how many mm are these measurements too long or too short?

3 Measure each of the lines below, **c, d, e, f** and **g**, in mm.
The mm is a very small unit, so care must be taken to measure accurately.

4 Draw this table and record your measurements. Check them.

| length | line c | line d | line e | line f | line g |
|---|---|---|---|---|---|
| in mm | | | | | |
| in cm | | | | | |

5 Write the lines in order of length putting the longest first.

Find the total length in mm of
6 the longest and shortest lines
7 lines **e** and **g**    8 lines **c** and **e**.

Find the difference in mm between:
9 the shortest and longest lines
10 lines **e** and **g**    11 lines **d** and **f**.

Find the length in mm of a line
12 three times as long as line **g**
13 four times as long as line **f**
14 six times as long as line **e**
15 $\frac{1}{3}$ of line **d**    16 $\frac{1}{4}$ of line **f**.
17 Check and correct the measurements in **6** to **16**.
Write them in cm.

18 a Write the length of line **c** above to the nearest cm.
   b Compare it with its measurement in mm.
   c Find by how many mm the measurement to the nearest cm is too long or too short.

19 In the same way, find the difference for each of the lines **d, e, f** and **g**.

Write each of these measurements to the nearest cm.
20 18 cm 7 mm    21 21 cm 2 mm
22 195 mm    23 109 mm
24 175 mm    25 203 mm
26 Find the differences in mm between the actual measurements and those to the nearest cm.

Measurements of lines are shown like this

82 mm

27 Draw lines of the following lengths and show the measurement of each.
You will need a pencil with a sharp point.
58 mm    92 mm    140 mm
7.6 cm    15.3 cm    20 cm

# Length   centimetres and millimetres

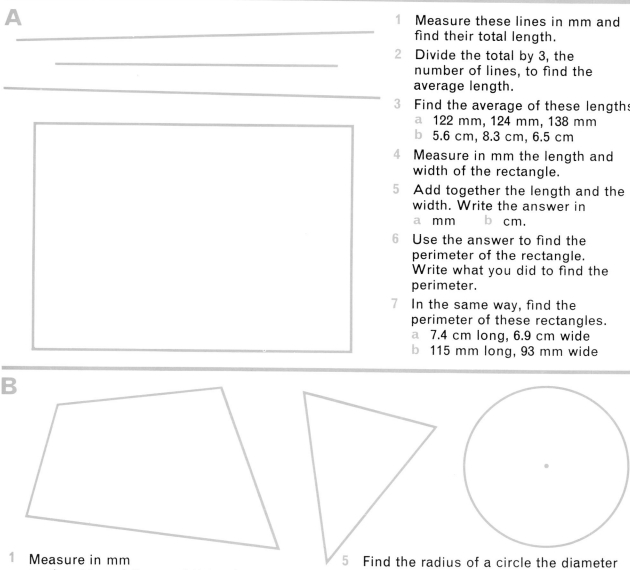

**A**

1   Measure these lines in mm and find their total length.

2   Divide the total by 3, the number of lines, to find the average length.

3   Find the average of these lengths.
   a   122 mm, 124 mm, 138 mm
   b   5.6 cm, 8.3 cm, 6.5 cm

4   Measure in mm the length and width of the rectangle.

5   Add together the length and the width. Write the answer in
   a   mm       b   cm.

6   Use the answer to find the perimeter of the rectangle. Write what you did to find the perimeter.

7   In the same way, find the perimeter of these rectangles.
   a   7.4 cm long, 6.9 cm wide
   b   115 mm long, 93 mm wide

**B**

1   Measure in mm
   a   the sides of the quadrilateral
   b   the sides of the triangle.

2   Find the perimeter of each. Write the answers
   a   in mm       b   in cm and mm       c   in cm.

3   What is the perimeter in cm of:
   a   a quadrilateral with sides double the length of those in the drawing
   b   a triangle with sides measuring 79 mm, 4.8 cm and 6 cm 7 mm?

4   Measure the diameter of the circle in mm. Find its radius and check by measuring.

5   Find the radius of a circle the diameter of which is:
   a   94 mm       b   3 cm 8 mm       c   15.6 cm.

6   Find the diameter of a circle the radius of which is:
   a   2 cm 5 mm       b   $20\frac{1}{2}$ cm       c   87 mm.

Write each of the following answers in mm and then in cm.

7   4.6 cm + 39 mm + 2.7 cm

8   a   250 mm − 103 mm       b   10.4 cm − 8.5 cm

9   a   53 mm × 8       b   6.7 cm × 10

10   a   224 mm ÷ 7       b   28.8 cm ÷ 9

# Length metres and centimetres

## A

| 1 metre (m)=100 centimetres (cm) |

Find how many cm there are in:

1 a 2 m 30 cm    b 5 m 80 cm    c 3 m 6 cm

2 a $6\frac{1}{4}$ m    b 9 m 4 cm    c $\frac{27}{100}$ m.

Change these measurements to m and cm.

3 a 690 cm    b 313 cm    c $2\frac{1}{2}$ m

4 a $3\frac{7}{10}$ m    b 509 cm    c 210 cm

Another way of writing m and cm is to **separate them by a point** and write the answers as m.

e.g. 237 cm = 2m 37 cm = 2.37 m

Complete these tables.

| | m | cm | | metres |
|---|---|---|---|---|
| 5   428 cm = | | | = | |
| 6   370 cm = | | | = | |
| 7   74 cm = | | | = | |
| 8   806 cm = | | | = | |
| 9   1045 cm = | | | = | |

Change the following to cm.

10 a 2.76 m    b 7.04 m    c 5.10 m

11 a 13.90 m    b 18.32 m    c 9.5 m

12 a 30.09 m    b 10.7 m    c 27.85 m

## B Estimating lengths by paces, foot-lengths, spans

1 Susan paced the length of a wall. It was 7 paces long. Her pace measured 45 cm. What was Susan's estimate of its length in:
a cm    b m and cm    c m?

2 The width of a corridor was 9 foot-lengths. Find its approximate width in m if 1 foot-length measured 18 cm.

3 The height of a cupboard is 8 spans. Estimate its height in cm if 1 span measures 15 cm.

Estimate the lengths and heights below in:
a m and cm    b m.

4 50 paces each measuring 70 cm

5 8 spans each measuring 17 cm

6 16 foot-lengths each measuring 20 cm

## C

1 Find the length of your own pace. Get a metre ruler marked in cm.

2 In the playground, mark a starting line with chalk and from it walk forward 10 ordinary paces.

3 Mark the distance and measure it to the nearest m.

4 Write and complete:
10 paces measure ☐ m or ☐ cm.
1 pace measures ☐ cm.

For estimating shorter distances, the foot-length is a useful unit.

5 From the starting line, go forward heel to toe for 10 lengths of your foot.

6 Mark the distance and measure it to the nearest cm.

7 Write and complete:
10 foot-lengths measure ☐ cm
1 foot-length measures ☐ cm.

8 In the same way, find the length in cm of your span. This measure is particularly useful in estimating heights.

9 Use the length of your pace, foot-length or span to estimate the following lengths or heights. Then measure in m or cm.

First draw this table and keep a record of the measurements.

| | estimate m or cm | measure m or cm | error +or— |
|---|---|---|---|
| **door** width height **window** | | | |

| | |
|---|---|
| **door** | width, height |
| **window** | height from floor, width |
| **table** | length, width, height |
| **desk** | length, width, height |
| **corridor** | length, width |

10  Measure to the nearest cm the length, width and height of a brick.

11 Find the approximate height of a wall by counting the bricks and allowing 1 cm for each row of mortar.

# Length   metres, centimetres and millimetres

**A**

| 1 metre (m) = 1000 millimetres (mm) |
|---|

Find how many mm there are in:

1   a   $2\frac{3}{4}$ m     b   1 m 870 mm    c   4 m 70 mm

2   a   1 m 5 mm    b   $\frac{7}{10}$ m        c   $\frac{3}{1000}$ m.

Change these measurements to m and mm.

3   a   2200 mm    b   1095 mm    c   3420 mm

4   a   5125 mm    b   6040 mm    c   $1\frac{3}{10}$m

5   a   795 mm     b   936 mm     c   $2\frac{7}{1000}$ m

Another way of writing m and mm is to **separate them by a point** and write the answers as m.

e.g. 1294 mm = 1 m 294 mm = 1.294 m

Complete these tables.

| | m | mm | | metres |
|---|---|---|---|---|
| 6   3185   mm = | | | = | |
| 7   1605   mm = | | | = | |
| 8    960   mm = | | | = | |
| 9   4092   mm = | | | = | |
| 10   5370   mm = | | | = | |

Change the following to mm.

11   a   1.428 m    b   0.916 m    c   3.027 m

12   a   2.803 m    b   0.605 m    c   9.005 m

13   a   6.070 m    b   0.009 m    c   7.100 m

**B**

Length measurements are usually expressed in metres or millimetres.

Write the answers   a   in mm   b   in m.

1   37 mm + 85 mm + 139 mm

2   365 mm + 492 mm + 359 mm

3   844 mm − 387 mm

4   506 mm − 198 mm

5   a   176 mm × 8     b   308 mm × 5

6   a   $\frac{1}{4}$ of 176 mm    b   972 mm ÷ 9

Write the answers   a   in m   b   in mm.

7   1.890 m + 0.376 m + 2.058 m

8   0.685 m + 0.730 m + 0.915 m

9   2.460 m − 1.875 m

10   10.000 m − 9.165 m

11   a   1.080 m × 6     b   0.315 m × 4

12   a   $\frac{1}{5}$ of 1.365 m    b   $\frac{1}{6}$ of 2.004 m

**C**

Write each of the following to the nearest m.

1   a   3600 mm     b   2870 mm

2   a   4504 mm     b   5490 mm

3   a   9850 mm     b   765 mm

| Recent competitions | | |
|---|---|---|
| event | men | women |
| High jump | 2.18 m | 1.90 m |
| Long jump | 8.07 m | 6.76 m |

4   Measure and mark on the wall, the heights jumped by the man and the woman.

5   Measure on the floor the distances jumped by the man and the woman.

6   By how many mm was the man's long jump greater than the woman's?

7   Find out all you can about the Olympic Games. When and where do the next games take place?

The measurements of the caravan as given in the catalogue are length 3098 mm, width 2000 mm, height 2450 mm.

8   Write each measurement in m.

9   Mark on the floor your estimate of the length and width of the caravan. Check the estimates by measuring.

10   By how many mm is the length greater than the width?

11   The length of the caravan and the tow bar is 3.897 m. Find the length of the tow bar in mm.

12   By how many mm are the length and width of the caravan greater than a room which measures $2\frac{1}{2}$ m by $1\frac{3}{4}$ m?

# Fractions

**A** Make sure you understand the diagram, then use it to help in answering the questions.

| whole one | | | | | | | |
|---|---|---|---|---|---|---|---|
| $\frac{1}{2}$ | | | | $\frac{1}{2}$ | | | |
| $\frac{1}{4}$ | | $\frac{1}{4}$ | | $\frac{1}{4}$ | | $\frac{1}{4}$ | |
| $\frac{1}{8}$ | $\frac{1}{8}$ | $\frac{1}{8}$ | $\frac{1}{8}$ | $\frac{1}{8}$ | $\frac{1}{8}$ | $\frac{1}{8}$ | $\frac{1}{8}$ |
| $\frac{1}{3}$ | | $\frac{1}{3}$ | | $\frac{1}{3}$ | | | |
| $\frac{1}{6}$ | $\frac{1}{6}$ | $\frac{1}{6}$ | $\frac{1}{6}$ | $\frac{1}{6}$ | $\frac{1}{6}$ | | |
| $\frac{1}{5}$ | $\frac{1}{5}$ | $\frac{1}{5}$ | $\frac{1}{5}$ | $\frac{1}{5}$ | | | |
| $\frac{1}{10}$ | $\frac{1}{10}$ | $\frac{1}{10}$ | $\frac{1}{10}$ | $\frac{1}{10}$ | $\frac{1}{10}$ | $\frac{1}{10}$ | $\frac{1}{10}$ $\frac{1}{10}$ $\frac{1}{10}$ |

Which of these fractions is the greater?

1 $\frac{1}{5}$ or $\frac{1}{4}$  2 $\frac{1}{2}$ or $\frac{2}{5}$  3 $\frac{2}{3}$ or $\frac{1}{2}$

4 $\frac{1}{8}$ or $\frac{1}{10}$  5 $\frac{3}{10}$ or $\frac{1}{4}$  6 $\frac{5}{6}$ or $\frac{3}{4}$

Put in the missing sign =, > or < in place of the ●.

7 $\frac{1}{6}$ ● $\frac{1}{5}$  8 $\frac{3}{5}$ ● $\frac{1}{2}$  9 $\frac{7}{10}$ ● $\frac{3}{5}$

10 $\frac{1}{8}$ ● $\frac{1}{6}$  11 $\frac{5}{6}$ ● $\frac{2}{3}$  12 $\frac{2}{3}$ ● $\frac{4}{6}$

13 $\frac{1}{4}$ ● $\frac{3}{8}$  14 $\frac{3}{4}$ ● $\frac{5}{8}$  15 $\frac{7}{8}$ ● $\frac{5}{6}$

By how many:

16 tenths is $\frac{1}{2}$ greater than $\frac{3}{10}$

17 eighths is $\frac{3}{4}$ less than $\frac{7}{8}$

18 sixths is $\frac{1}{3}$ less than $\frac{5}{6}$

19 tenths is $\frac{3}{5}$ greater than $\frac{1}{2}$?

Write these fractions in order, putting the largest first.

20 $\frac{1}{2}$, $\frac{3}{4}$, $\frac{3}{8}$  21 $\frac{1}{3}$, $\frac{1}{2}$, $\frac{1}{4}$  22 $\frac{7}{10}$, $\frac{1}{2}$, $\frac{3}{5}$

23 $\frac{1}{4}$, $\frac{1}{2}$, $\frac{1}{5}$  24 $\frac{1}{2}$, $\frac{5}{6}$, $\frac{2}{3}$  25 $\frac{2}{5}$, $\frac{3}{10}$, $\frac{3}{6}$

**B**

1 How many **eighths** are there in $\frac{1}{4}$? Write and complete: $\frac{1}{4}=\frac{\square}{8}$.

2 How many **sixths** are there in $\frac{1}{3}$? Write and complete: $\frac{1}{3}=\frac{\square}{6}$.

Copy the following fractions and put in the missing numerator or denominator.

3 $\frac{3}{4}=\frac{\square}{8}$  4 $\frac{3}{5}=\frac{\square}{10}$  5 $\frac{4}{5}=\frac{8}{\square}$

6 $\frac{2}{3}=\frac{\square}{6}$  7 $\frac{1}{2}=\frac{3}{\square}$  8 $\frac{1}{2}=\frac{5}{\square}$

Mark the answers.

> **Remember** When the **numerator** and the **denominator** of a fraction are **multiplied** by the **same number** the value of the fraction is unchanged.

9 Here is a set of equal fractions. $\{\frac{1}{2}, \frac{2}{4}, \frac{3}{6}, \dots\}$ The dots tell you that the members of the set go on and on. Write three more members of the set.

Write three more members of these sets of equal fractions.

10 $\{\frac{1}{3}, \frac{2}{6}, \frac{4}{12}, \dots\}$  11 $\{\frac{3}{4}, \frac{6}{8}, \frac{9}{12}, \dots\}$

12 $\{\frac{1}{5}, \frac{2}{10}, \frac{3}{15}, \dots\}$  13 $\{\frac{2}{3}, \frac{4}{6}, \frac{6}{9}, \dots\}$

**C** Copy the following fractions and put in the missing numerator or denominator.

1 $\frac{3}{6}=\frac{\square}{2}$  2 $\frac{5}{10}=\frac{\square}{2}$

3 $\frac{6}{8}=\frac{\square}{4}$  4 $\frac{8}{10}=\frac{4}{\square}$

5 $\frac{4}{6}=\frac{2}{\square}$  6 $\frac{6}{10}=\frac{3}{\square}$

Mark the answers.

> **Remember** When the **numerator** and the **denominator** of a fraction are **divided** by the **same number** the value of the fraction is unchanged.

The next process is called **cancelling**.

e.g. cancelling by 2

$\frac{14}{16} = \frac{14 \div 2}{16 \div 2} = \frac{7}{8}$

or $\frac{\overset{7}{\cancel{14}}}{\underset{8}{\cancel{16}}} = \frac{7}{8}$

Cancel each of these fractions

by 2  7 $\frac{10}{12}$  8 $\frac{6}{10}$  9 $\frac{14}{20}$

by 3  10 $\frac{9}{12}$  11 $\frac{6}{15}$  12 $\frac{15}{18}$

by 5  13 $\frac{10}{15}$  14 $\frac{20}{25}$  15 $\frac{5}{20}$

by 10.  16 $\frac{10}{30}$  17 $\frac{20}{50}$  18 $\frac{90}{100}$

# Fractions

**A** Cancel these fractions by dividing the numerator and the denominator by the same number.

1 $\frac{3}{15}$    2 $\frac{6}{12}$    3 $\frac{15}{20}$    4 $\frac{50}{100}$

By cancelling, complete the following.

5 $\frac{8}{16} = \frac{\square}{8} = \frac{\square}{4} = \frac{\square}{2}$    6 $\frac{8}{12} = \frac{\square}{6} = \frac{\square}{3}$

7 $\frac{16}{20} = \frac{\square}{10} = \frac{\square}{5}$    8 $\frac{12}{18} = \frac{\square}{9} = \frac{\square}{3}$

| $\frac{3}{4}$ | $\frac{5}{6}$ | $\frac{2}{3}$ | $\frac{3}{5}$ | $\frac{7}{10}$ | $\frac{5}{8}$ |
|---|---|---|---|---|---|

None of the fractions in the box can be cancelled.
Each is said to be in its **lowest terms**.

Cancel these fractions and write them in their lowest terms.

9 $\frac{4}{10}$    10 $\frac{4}{12}$    11 $\frac{12}{20}$    12 $\frac{30}{40}$

13 $\frac{9}{12}$    14 $\frac{10}{12}$    15 $\frac{10}{15}$    16 $\frac{70}{100}$

**B**

a What fraction of the whole one is one equal part?

b Write in its lowest terms the fraction of the whole one which is shaded; unshaded.

Write in the lowest terms what fraction of strip **X** is    a strip **Y**    b strip **Z**.

3 What fraction of strip **Y** is strip **Z**?

4 In a class of 24 there are 16 boys and 8 girls. What fraction, in its lowest terms, of the whole class are   a boys   b girls?

5 A piece of wood $\frac{1}{2}$ m long is cut into two pieces measuring 35 cm and 15 cm. What fraction, in its lowest terms, of the whole is each piece?

6 Write as fractions in their lowest terms:
   a  4 of 14                b  15 m of 40 m
   c  £6 of £18              d  75 g of 100 g.

**C** A whole number with a fraction is called a **mixed number**.

$4 + \frac{1}{2} = 4\frac{1}{2}$

$1 + \frac{3}{5} = 1\frac{3}{5}$

$2 + \frac{3}{4} = 2\frac{3}{4}$

1 How many halves in $4\frac{1}{2}$?
Write and complete:  $4\frac{1}{2} = \frac{\square}{2}$.

2 How many fifths in $1\frac{3}{5}$?
Write and complete:  $1\frac{3}{5} = \frac{\square}{5}$.

3 How many quarters in $2\frac{3}{4}$?
Write and complete:  $2\frac{3}{4} = \frac{\square}{4}$.
Mark the answers to examples **1**, **2** and **3**.

Notice that in each case the **numerator** is larger than the **denominator**.
Such fractions are **improper** fractions.

How many whole ones are there in:

4 15 thirds           5 32 eighths

6 18 halves           7 28 quarters

8 $\frac{60}{10}$              9 $\frac{36}{6}$?

Change the following improper fractions to mixed numbers.

10 $\frac{11}{10}$    11 $\frac{12}{5}$    12 $\frac{21}{8}$    13 $\frac{23}{6}$

14 $\frac{8}{3}$    15 $\frac{17}{4}$    16 $\frac{37}{10}$    17 $\frac{29}{3}$

Change the following mixed numbers to improper fractions.

18 $1\frac{4}{5}$    19 $4\frac{3}{4}$    20 $2\frac{5}{6}$    21 $5\frac{7}{8}$

22 $3\frac{3}{10}$    23 $5\frac{2}{3}$    24 $6\frac{7}{10}$    25 $8\frac{2}{5}$

Complete the following series.

26 $1\frac{1}{3}$,  $1\frac{2}{3}$,  $\square$,  $\square$,  $\square$,  3

27 $2\frac{7}{10}$,  $2\frac{4}{5}$,  $\square$,  $\square$,  $\square$,  $3\frac{1}{5}$

28 $4\frac{5}{8}$,  $4\frac{3}{4}$,  $\square$,  $\square$,  $\square$,  $5\frac{1}{4}$

Write as £s and pence.

29 $£7\frac{3}{10}$        30 $£14\frac{7}{10}$        31 $£8\frac{19}{100}$

Write as m and cm.

32 $3\frac{7}{10}$ m        33 $9\frac{59}{100}$ m        34 $12\frac{23}{100}$ m

# Fractions

**A**

The fractions in each of these sets have the same name or denominator. Put the fractions in each set in order, the smallest first.

1 $\{\frac{5}{12}, \frac{1}{12}, \frac{11}{12}, \frac{7}{12}\}$    2 $\{\frac{5}{16}, \frac{9}{16}, \frac{3}{16}, \frac{13}{16}\}$

3 $\{\frac{9}{10}, \frac{3}{10}, \frac{1}{10}, \frac{7}{10}\}$    4 $\{\frac{11}{20}, \frac{7}{20}, \frac{3}{20}, \frac{19}{20}\}$

Write the members of the following sets of fractions, changing them to the given denominator. Put the fractions in each set in order, the smallest first.

5 eighths     $\{\frac{1}{2}, \frac{1}{4}, \frac{3}{4}, \frac{5}{8}\}$

6 twelfths    $\{\frac{1}{2}, \frac{3}{4}, \frac{2}{3}, \frac{5}{6}\}$

7 tenths      $\{\frac{1}{2}, \frac{2}{5}, \frac{7}{10}, \frac{1}{5}\}$

8 sixteenths  $\{\frac{3}{4}, \frac{9}{16}, \frac{5}{8}, \frac{1}{2}\}$

9 fifteenths  $\{\frac{1}{3}, \frac{2}{5}, \frac{11}{15}, \frac{2}{3}\}$

**B**

1 What fraction of the whole one is coloured
   a black    b blue?

2 What fraction of the whole one is coloured?
   Write and complete: $\frac{1}{10} + \frac{3}{10} = \frac{\square}{10}$.
   Write this answer in its lowest terms.

In the same way, find the answers in their lowest terms to the following.

3 $\frac{3}{8} + \frac{1}{8}$     4 $\frac{7}{10} + \frac{1}{10}$     5 $\frac{1}{12} + \frac{5}{12}$

6 $\frac{2}{5} + \frac{1}{5}$     7 $\frac{3}{8} + \frac{3}{8}$      8 $\frac{9}{16} + \frac{3}{16}$

**Always make sure that answers are in their lowest terms.**

The answers to the following are improper fractions. Change them to **mixed numbers.**

9 $\frac{5}{8} + \frac{7}{8}$     10 $\frac{2}{5} + \frac{4}{5}$     11 $\frac{7}{12} + \frac{11}{12}$

12 $\frac{3}{10} + \frac{9}{10}$   13 $\frac{5}{6} + \frac{5}{6}$     14 $\frac{3}{4} + \frac{3}{4}$

To add **unlike** fractions, change them first to fractions with the **same denominator**.

15 $\frac{2}{3} + \frac{1}{6}$     16 $\frac{1}{4} + \frac{5}{8}$     17 $\frac{1}{6} + \frac{1}{2}$

18 $\frac{1}{10} + \frac{3}{5}$   19 $\frac{1}{2} + \frac{3}{10}$    20 $\frac{1}{2} + \frac{5}{12}$

**C**

1 What fraction of the whole one is shaded?

2 What fraction is unshaded?

3 Write and complete:

a $1 - \frac{5}{8} = \frac{\square}{8}$    b $1 - \frac{3}{8} = \frac{\square}{8}$.

Write the answers to the following.

4 $1 - \frac{5}{6}$     5 $1 - \frac{3}{4}$     6 $1 - \frac{7}{10}$

7 $1 - \frac{2}{3}$     8 $2 - \frac{4}{5}$     9 $3 - \frac{5}{8}$

10 $\frac{7}{10} - \frac{3}{10}$   11 $\frac{7}{8} - \frac{3}{8}$   12 $\frac{9}{16} - \frac{5}{16}$

13 $\frac{5}{6} - \frac{1}{6}$    14 $\frac{7}{12} - \frac{3}{12}$   15 $\frac{9}{10} - \frac{7}{10}$

To subtract **unlike** fractions, change them first to fractions with the **same denominator**.

16 $\frac{2}{3} - \frac{1}{6}$     17 $\frac{1}{2} - \frac{1}{3}$     18 $\frac{7}{8} - \frac{1}{2}$

19 $\frac{3}{4} - \frac{5}{8}$     20 $\frac{7}{10} - \frac{2}{5}$    21 $\frac{1}{2} - \frac{2}{5}$

22 $\frac{4}{5} - \frac{1}{10}$    23 $\frac{1}{4} - \frac{1}{12}$   24 $\frac{11}{16} - \frac{1}{2}$

**D**

Write the missing signs =, > or < in place of the ●.

1 $\frac{3}{4} ● \frac{5}{8}$     2 $\frac{7}{12} ● \frac{2}{3}$     3 $\frac{5}{6} ● \frac{2}{3}$

4 $\frac{2}{5} ● \frac{1}{2}$     5 $\frac{3}{8} ● \frac{3}{16}$     6 $\frac{3}{4} ● \frac{15}{20}$

7 6 metres of wire is cut into 8 equal pieces. What fraction of 1 m is each piece?

8 What fraction of   a £1·00 is 15p
   b 1 kg is 300g    c $\frac{1}{2}$ ℓ is 200 mℓ?

9 $\frac{1}{8}$ kg of chocolates cost 25p.
   Find the cost of   a $\frac{1}{2}$ kg    b 1$\frac{1}{4}$ kg.

10 A boy spent $\frac{5}{6}$ of his money. He had 35p left. How much had he at first?

11 John spent $\frac{1}{4}$ of his money and then $\frac{1}{3}$ of the remainder. What fraction
   a has he spent    b has he left?

12 Find the difference in cm between $\frac{2}{5}$ of 1 metre and $\frac{3}{10}$ of 1 metre.

13 2$\frac{1}{4}$ m of cloth cost £3·60.
   Find the cost of   a $\frac{1}{4}$ m    b 1 m.

14 A girl had 10 out of 15 examples correct. What fraction had she wrong?

# Shapes

**A**

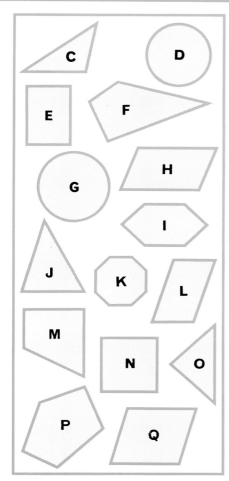

Shapes are usually put into sets according to the number of sides they have. Each set has its own name.

> All shapes with straight sides are called **polygons**.
> Some polygons have special names.
> Polygons with three sides are called **triangles**.
> Polygons with four sides are called **quadrilaterals**.

In the box there are 15 different shapes, **C** to **Q**.

Write the members of each of the following sets, using the shape letters only.

1   T = {triangles}
2   Q = {quadrilaterals}
3   Y = {shapes which are not polygons}
4   Z = {shapes with more than four sides}
5   Shape **P** has five sides. It is called a **pentagon**.
    What is the name of shape **I**; shape **K**?
    Check your answers.
6   Copy and complete the table. Write in the name and the number of sides and angles in each of the given shapes.

| shape | name | sides | angles |
|-------|------|-------|--------|
| C     |      |       |        |
| E     |      |       |        |
| G     |      |       |        |
| I     |      |       |        |
| N     |      |       |        |

7   Name the shapes in the box which are not polygons.

**B**

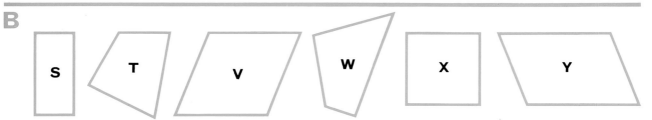

1   All the shapes above are quadrilaterals.
    Give the reason.

    Which of these shapes have:
2   four sides equal in length
3   the opposite sides equal in length
4   the opposite sides parallel
5   four right angles
6   no equal sides and no equal angles?

7   Give the letter of the shape which is:
    a   a square     b   a rectangle.
8   Shape **V** is called a **rhombus**.
    It has four equal sides.
    Why is it not a square?
9   Shape **Y** is called a **parallelogram**.
    Its pairs of opposite sides are equal.
    Why is it not a rectangle?

    **T** and **W** are quadrilaterals.

# Shapes quadrilaterals

## A

1. On cm squared paper, draw a large square, 10 cm side at least. Cut it out.
2. Fold it in half along a vertical fold. One half must fit on the other half.
3. Now fold the square in half
   a along a horizontal fold
   b along the diagonals.
   One half must fit on the other half.
4. Mark each fold by a dotted line.
5. Why are these lines lines of symmetry?
6. At which point in the square do all the lines of symmetry cross?
7. Write and complete: A square has ☐ lines of symmetry.
8. Repeat exercise **A1** to **6** using squares of different sizes.

## B

1. On cm squared paper, draw a large rectangle. Cut it out.
2. Fold the rectangle in half along
   a a vertical fold      b a horizontal fold.
   One half must fit on the other half.
3. Mark each fold by a dotted line.

4. Why are these lines lines of symmetry?
5. Test by folding if the diagonals of the rectangle are lines of symmetry.
6. Describe how to find the centre point.
7. Fold the rectangle in half. What do you learn about the opposite sides?
8. Write and complete: A rectangle has ☐ lines of symmetry.
9. Repeat exercise **B1** to **7** using rectangles of different sizes and shapes.

## C

1. How does a parallelogram differ from a rectangle?
2. On cm squared paper, draw a large parallelogram. Cut it out.
3. Try to fold the parallelogram in half so that one half fits exactly on the other half.

**parallelogram**

4. Write and complete: A parallelogram has ☐ lines of symmetry.
5. Repeat exercise **C2** and **3** using parallelograms of different sizes and shapes.

## D

This chart will help you to remember facts about special kinds of quadrilaterals.

| Square | Rectangle | Rhombus | Parallelogram |
|---|---|---|---|
| 4 equal sides<br>4 right angles<br>4 lines of symmetry | Opposite sides equal<br>4 right angles<br>2 lines of symmetry | 4 equal sides<br>Opposite sides parallel<br>Angles not right angles<br>2 lines of symmetry | Opposite sides<br>equal and parallel<br>Angles not right angles<br>No line of symmetry |
| **Diagonals equal in length** | | **Diagonals not equal in length** | |

# Shapes   quadrilaterals

**A**

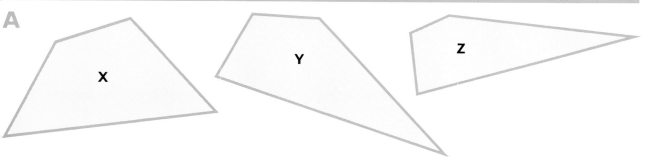

1   How many:
     a   sides     b   angles
    has each of the shapes **X**, **Y** and **Z**?

    The shapes are **quadrilaterals** but they
    do not belong to any of the special sets
    you have learnt about so far.

2   In each shape, what can you say about:
     a   the lengths of the sides
     b   the sizes of the angles?

3   Are any pairs of opposite sides parallel?

4   On cm squared paper draw three large
    quadrilaterals each with sides and
    angles of different sizes.

5   Draw the diagonals in each.
    Measure them in mm.
    What do you find out about the diagonals
    in each of these quadrilaterals?

6   Cut out the quadrilaterals.
    Try to fold each of them in half so that
    one half fits exactly on the other.
    How many lines of symmetry can you find?

**B**

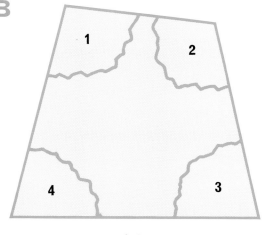

### Angles in quadrilaterals

The four angles of a square or a rectangle, when
added together, make **4 right angles**.

You can now discover how many right angles are
made by the four angles of any quadrilateral.

1   On a piece of gummed paper draw a large
    quadrilateral. Cut it out.

2   Mark the angles **1**, **2**, **3** and **4**, as shown.

3   Tear off each of the angles, fit them together and
    stick them on a sheet of paper.

4   Draw other quadrilaterals of different sizes
    and shapes.
    Repeat the exercise with each shape.

5   Write and complete:

    The four angles of any quadrilateral together
    equal ☐ right angles or ☐°.

6   On cm squared paper, draw a large rhombus and
    a large parallelogram.
    Tear off the four angles of each. Fit them together.
    How many degrees are in the four angles of
     a   a rhombus     b   a parallelogram?

# Mass   kilograms and grams

**A**

1  Get a pair of scales and the masses.
   Make a list of the masses in order,
   putting the heaviest first.

2  Feel each mass in your hand. Then
   practise with a partner picking them up
   in any order and naming them without
   looking at them.

3  Collect three articles each of which you
   estimate has a mass of about 1 kg.

4  Put each article in turn on the scale pan
   and find if its mass is heavier or lighter
   than 1 kg.

5  a  Estimate 500 g of sand. Put it in a bag.
   b  Find, by weighing, if your estimate is
      greater or less than 500 g.
   c  Make the mass exactly 500 g.

6  In the same way, estimate
   a  200 g    b  100 g of sand.
   Check the estimate by weighing, and
   then make each quantity the exact mass.

7  Collect several articles which have a
   mass less than 1 kg. Weigh each article
   in g as accurately as possible.

8  Collect some articles which have a mass
   heavier than 1 kg, e.g. parcels of books,
   bricks, tins of sand, etc.
   Draw this table for recording your results.

| article | estimate to $\frac{1}{2}$ kg | mass kg   g | error +or− |
|---------|------------------------------|-------------|------------|
|         |                              |             |            |

9  First estimate to $\frac{1}{2}$ kg the mass of each
   article and then weigh it in kg and g.

10 Show by + or − whether the estimate is
   too heavy or too light.

   5 kg, 2 kg, 1 kg, 500 g, 200 g, 100 g, 50 g

   Which of the masses shown above,
   together balance the following masses?

11 a  $1\frac{1}{2}$ kg     b  2 kg 250 g   c  600 g
12 a  5 kg 300 g  b  6 kg 800 g  c  3 kg 150 g

**B**

   **1 kilogram (kg)=1000 grams (g)**

Find how many g there are in:
1  a  2 kg        b  $\frac{1}{2}$ kg       c  $\frac{1}{4}$ kg
2  a  $2\frac{3}{4}$ kg      b  1 kg 400 g    c  3 kg 50 g.

Change these masses to kg and g.
3  a  6000 g      b  4800 g      c  1020 g
4  a  920 g       b  3560 g      c  5170 g

Another way of writing kg and g is to
**separate them by a point** and write the
answers as kg.
e.g. 1750 g = 1 kg 750 g = 1.750 kg

Complete these tables.

|        | kg | g |   | kilograms |
|--------|----|----|----|-----------|
| 5  2370 g = |  |  | = |  |
| 6  4450 g = |  |  | = |  |
| 7  3900 g = |  |  | = |  |
| 8  820 g = |  |  | = |  |
| 9  5040 g = |  |  | = |  |
| 10 1030 g = |  |  | = |  |

Change the following to g.
11 a  1.300 kg    b  3.750 kg    c  2.080 kg
12 a  0.450 kg    b  0.090 kg    c  0.005 kg

What fraction, in its lowest terms, of 1kg is
13 a  500 g       b  250 g       c  750 g?

What fraction, in its lowest terms, of 1kg is
14 a  100 g       b  300 g       c  900 g?

What fraction, in its lowest terms, of 1kg is
15 a  200 g       b  600 g       c  800 g?

Write the following to the nearest kg.
16 a  2 kg 450 g         b  4 kg 870 g
17 a  $3\frac{7}{10}$ kg          b  $7\frac{3}{10}$ kg
18 a  1.950 kg           b  5.250 kg

Write the answers only.
19 1 kg−350 g        20  1 kg−560 g
21 $\frac{1}{2}$ kg−180 g        22  0.5 kg−130 g
23 1.5 kg−900 g       24  0.25 kg−190 g

# Mass kilograms and grams

## A

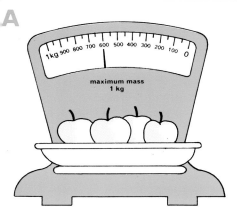

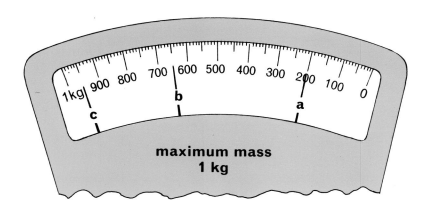

The picture shows a type of scales often used in shops for weighing fruit, meats, etc.

The goods to be weighed are placed in the pan.

The pointer which moves across the dial gives the mass.

You must learn to read many different dials.

1 Name the units shown on the dial above.

2 What is the mass shown by the pointer?

This diagram shows the dial on the same scales but enlarged.

3 What is the greatest mass in g which can be recorded on the dial?

4 What mass is shown by:
a the large divisions
b the small divisions?

5 Read the masses shown by the pointers **a**, **b** and **c**.

6 By how many g is mass **a** less than $\frac{1}{2}$ kg?

7 How many g greater than $\frac{1}{2}$ kg is mass **b**; mass **c**?

8 What does **maximum mass 1 kg** mean?

## B

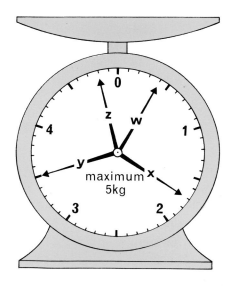

This picture shows another type of scales with a different dial.

1 What is the greatest mass which can be recorded on the dial?

2 What mass in g does each small division represent?

3 Read the masses shown by the pointers **w, x, y** and **z**.
Check the answers.

4 By how many kg and g is:
a mass **x** greater than 1 kg,
b mass **y** less than 5 kg,
c mass **z** greater than mass **y**?

5 Write each of the masses to the nearest $\frac{1}{2}$ kg.

# Mass   kilograms and grams

**A**

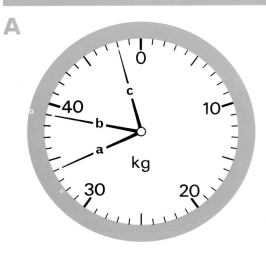

The diagram shows the dial on a weighing-machine suitable for finding the masses of children.
Find:

1 the maximum mass which can be recorded on the dial

2 the mass shown by one small division

3 the mass of each of the three children shown by the pointers **a**, **b** and **c**

4 the difference between the masses of the heaviest and lightest child.

5 Get the school weighing-machine.
Weigh yourself and your partner.
Who is heavier and by how many kg?

The mass of each of five children is given in the table.

| name | mass in kg |
|---|---|
| Joan | $37\frac{1}{2}$ |
| Molly | 42 |
| Peter | 50 |
| Susan | $39\frac{1}{2}$ |
| David | 46 |

6 Write their names in order of their masses, putting the heaviest first.

7 Find their total mass. Check the answer.

8 Divide this total by 5, the number of children, to find the **average mass**.

9 By how many kg is Peter above the average?

10 By how many kg is Joan below the average?

**B** Write and complete:

1 750 g + 200 g + 1 kg 150 g = ☐ kg ☐ g = ☐ g

2 2.300 kg + 3.850 kg = ☐ kg = ☐ g.

3 Find the difference in g between
  a 2 kg 450 g and 1 kg 800 g
  b 3.400 kg and 2.650 kg.

4 a 320 g × 7   Give the answer in kg.
  b 1 kg 240 g × 9
    Give the answer in kg and g.
  c 1.650 kg × 8
    Give the answer in kg and g.

5 The total mass of 6 parcels is 25.200 kg.
Find the average mass in kg and g.

6 Find the average of these masses.
  a 340 g, 280 g, 310 g and 290 g
  b 3 kg 100 g, 2 kg 600 g and 2 kg 400 g

7 How many packets of tea each weighing 400 g can be made from 5.200 kg?

8 Write the following to the nearest $\frac{1}{2}$ kg.
  a 5 kg 720 g   b 9.300 kg

Find the cost of:

9 500 g at 84p per kg

10 1.500 kg at 68p per kg

11 200 g at 70p per kg

12 14.250 kg at £1 per kg

13 3 kg 750 g at 48p per kg

14 100 g at 55p per $\frac{1}{2}$ kg

15 250 g at 36p per $\frac{1}{2}$ kg

16 200 g at 20p per $\frac{1}{2}$ kg

17 600 g at 15p per $\frac{1}{2}$ kg

18 1 kg 100 g at 40p per $\frac{1}{2}$ kg.

Which of the given masses is a good estimate for the mass of:

| | | | |
|---|---|---|---|
| 19 a chicken | 50 g | 15 kg | 2 kg |
| 20 a large apple | 10 g | 200 g | 7 kg |
| 21 a joint of meat | 100 g | $1\frac{1}{2}$ kg | 40 kg |
| 22 a man? | 75 kg | 20 kg | 200 kg |

# Decimal notation

**A**

| Th | H | T | U |
|----|---|---|---|
|    |   |   |   |
|    |   |   |   |
|    |   |   |   |
|    |   |   |   |
|    |   |   |   |
|    |   |   |   |
|    |   |   |   |

Draw these number columns.

Write the following numbers, making sure that each figure is placed in the correct column.

1. 208
2. 8430
3. 2006
4. 59
5. 5762
6. six hundred and four
7. three thousand and twenty-eight
8. seven hundred and eleven
9. five thousand and forty
10. two thousand eight hundred and thirty-one

**B** **Watch the numbers getting bigger.**

| Th | H | T | U |  |  | H | T | U |
|----|---|---|---|--|--|---|---|---|
|    |   | 6 | 0 | ←— 10× — |  |   |   | 6 |
|    | 5 | 1 | 0 | ←— 10× — |  |   | 5 | 1 |
|  2 | 3 | 4 | 0 | ←— 10× — |  | 2 | 3 | 4 |

Move the numbers **one place** to the **left**.

Put 0 in the empty place.

Each number is then 10 times bigger.

1. Make each of these numbers 10 times bigger.
   a  9  b  67  c  350
2. Multiply each of these numbers by 10.
   a  13  b  90  c  208

| Th | H | T | U |  |  | H | T | U |
|----|---|---|---|--|--|---|---|---|
|    | 7 | 0 | 0 | ←— 100× — |  |   |   | 7 |
|  9 | 5 | 0 | 0 | ←— 100× — |  |   | 9 | 5 |

Move the numbers **two places** to the **left**.

Put 00 in the empty places.

Each number is then 100 times bigger.

3. Make each of these numbers 100 times bigger.
   a  5  b  27  c  80
4. Multiply each of these numbers by 100.
   a  8  b  30  c  74

| Th | H | T | U |  |  | H | T | U |
|----|---|---|---|--|--|---|---|---|
|  4 | 0 | 0 | 0 | ←— 1000× — |  |   |   | 4 |
|  8 | 0 | 0 | 0 | ←— 1000× — |  |   |   | 8 |

Move the numbers **three places** to the **left**.

Put 000 in the empty places.

Each number is then 1000 times bigger.

5. Make each of these numbers 1000 times bigger.
   a  3  b  6  c  10
6. Multiply each of these numbers by 1000.
   a  7  b  9  c  14

**C** How many times is:
1. 30 bigger than 3
2. 550 bigger than 55
3. 700 bigger than 7
4. 2000 bigger than 2
5. 8900 bigger than 89
6. 1260 bigger than 126
7. 340 bigger than 34
8. 7000 bigger than 7
9. 1100 bigger than 11
10. 100 bigger than 10?

11. $\overset{x\ \ \ y}{3333}$  How many times is the 3 at $x$ greater than the 3 at $y$?

12. $\overset{x\ \ \ \ \ y}{9999}$  How many times is the 9 at $x$ greater than the 9 at $y$?

# Decimal notation

## A Watch the numbers getting smaller.

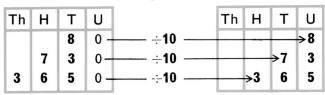

| Th | H | T | U |
|----|---|---|---|
|    |   | 8 | 0 |
|    | 7 | 3 | 0 |
| 3  | 6 | 5 | 0 |

÷10 → 8
÷10 → 7 3
÷10 → 3 6 5

| Th | H | T | U |
|----|---|---|---|
|    |   |   | 8 |
|    |   | 7 | 3 |
|    | 3 | 6 | 5 |

Move the numbers **one place** to the **right**.
Each number is then 10 times smaller.

1 Make these numbers 10 times smaller.
  a 40    b 130    c 650    d 1100    e 3070

2 Divide each of these numbers by 10.
  a 70    b 280    c 900    d 1960    e 2050

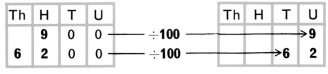

| Th | H | T | U |
|----|---|---|---|
|    | 9 | 0 | 0 |
| 6  | 2 | 0 | 0 |

÷100 → 9
÷100 → 6 2

| Th | H | T | U |
|----|---|---|---|
|    |   |   | 9 |
|    | 6 | 2 |   |

Move the numbers **two places** to the **right**.
Each number is then 100 times smaller.

3 Make these numbers 100 times smaller.
  a 200    b 1000    c 1700    d 5200

4 Divide each of these numbers by 100.
  a 500    b 2000    c 4900    d 8000

| Th | H | T | U |
|----|---|---|---|
| 1  | 0 | 0 | 0 |
| 5  | 0 | 0 | 0 |

÷1000 → 1
÷1000 → 5

| Th | H | T | U |
|----|---|---|---|
|    |   |   | 1 |
|    |   |   | 5 |

Move the numbers **three places** to the **right**.
Each number is then 1000 times smaller.

5 Make these numbers 1000 times smaller.
  a 7000    b 10 000    c 15 000

6 Divide each of these numbers by 1000.
  a 9000    b 3000    c 20 000

When writing 10 000 and above, leave a small space to separate the thousands from the hundreds e.g. 10 187.

## B How many times smaller than:

1 70 is 7
2 500 is 5
3 4000 is 4
4 360 is 36
5 1000 is 10
6 1300 is 13
7 1420 is 142
8 3050 is 305
9 1000 is 100
10 8000 is 8?

11 $\overset{y\ \ x}{6666}$ How many times is the 6 at x smaller than the 6 at y?

12 $\overset{y\ \ x}{8888}$ How many times is the 8 at x smaller than the 8 at y?

## C

| Th | H | T | U |
|----|---|---|---|
| 1  | 1 | 1 | 1 |

to the right →

| Th | H | T | U | tenths |
|----|---|---|---|--------|
| 1  | 1 | 1 | 1 | 1      |

to the right →

1 By how many times is the value of the figure decreased each time it is moved **one place to the right**?

In this diagram, the figure 1 in the **units** column is moved one further place **to the right** so its value is again 10 times smaller. $1 \div 10 = \frac{1}{10}$ **one tenth**

2 If the figure in the units column was  a 3    b 7, what would be its value moved one place to the right?

# Decimal fractions tenths

**A** Write the numbers shown in the columns.

| H | T | U | t |
|---|---|---|---|
| 1 |   |   | 7 | 6 |
| 2 |   | 4 | 2 | 3 |
| 3 |   | 7 | 9 | 2 |
| 4 | 5 | 0 | 8 | 4 |
| 5 |   | 9 | 0 | 7 |
| 6 | 8 | 0 | 0 | 5 |
| 7 |   | 1 | 5 | 8 |
| 8 | 2 | 5 | 0 | 1 |

The first two are done for you.

7 units 6 tenths $=7\frac{6}{10}$

4 tens 2 units 3 tenths $=42\frac{3}{10}$

Draw similar columns and write in these numbers.

9  $8\frac{7}{10}$ 

12  $104\frac{9}{10}$

10  $27\frac{3}{10}$ 

13  $420\frac{2}{10}$

11  $70\frac{4}{10}$ 

14  $12\frac{6}{10}$

In exercises **1** to **8** above, **tenths** are written in words and as vulgar fractions. Usually **tenths** are written as **decimal fractions**.
Decimal fractions are based on the **tens number system** as shown in the diagram.

| Th | H | T | U | t<br>tenths |
|---|---|---|---|---|
| 1 | 1 | 1 | 1 $\bullet$ | 1 |
| **whole ones** | | | $\bullet$ **parts** | |

increases 10 times for each place

$\longleftarrow$

decreases 10 times for each place

$\longrightarrow$

The decimal point separates the **whole ones** from the **parts of a whole one**.
e.g. 1 tenth $\frac{1}{10}=0.1$
which is read as "nought point one".
2 whole ones and 3 tenths $2\frac{3}{10}=2.3$
which is read as "two point three".
Write the following as decimal fractions.

15  $\frac{3}{10}$ 

16  $8\frac{2}{10}$ 

17  $10\frac{8}{10}$

18  $27\frac{7}{10}$ 

19  $105\frac{4}{10}$ 

20  $200\frac{9}{10}$

Write as decimal fractions, in words and figures, the number shown on each abacus.

21

22

23

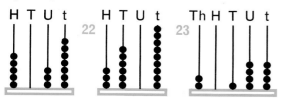

**B**

> **Remember**
> The figure in the **first place** after the decimal point is the number of **tenths**.

Write the following as decimals.

1  3 units and 7 tenths

2  20 units and 3 tenths

3  5 tens, 2 units and 4 tenths

4  1 hundred, 9 units and 6 tenths

5  4 hundreds, 5 units and 8 tenths

6  a  51 tenths          b  77 tenths

7  a  122 tenths         b  308 tenths

8  a  151 tenths         b  109 tenths

Write and complete:

9  9.2 = ☐ units ☐ tenths = ☐ tenths

10  37.6 = ☐ tens ☐ units ☐ tenths = ☐ tenths

11  41.9 = ☐ units ☐ tenths = ☐ tenths

12  a  24.7= ☐ tenths    b  38.2= ☐ tenths

13  a  170.8= ☐ tenths   b  305.9= ☐ tenths.

**C** Write each of the following as a vulgar fraction or a mixed number.

When possible, cancel the fraction.
e.g. $0.2 = \frac{2}{10} = \frac{1}{5}$;     $4.6 = 4\frac{6}{10} = 4\frac{3}{5}$

1  a  0.3        b  0.8        c  0.7

2  a  5.4        b  14.6       c  11.5

Write the value of the figure underlined in each of the numbers.

3  a  2̲09.4      b  38.5̲      c  89̲4

4  a  6̲13.8      b  6̲0.9      c  552.7̲

5  a  2̲076      b  520̲8      c  900.6̲

By moving each figure one place to the left, multiply the numbers by 10.

6  a  0.6        b  0.1        c  0.9

7  a  1.4        b  3.7        c  8.2

8  a  13.3       b  40.5       c  108.8

By moving each figure one place to the right, divide the numbers by 10.

9  a  4          b  7          c  5

10  a  19        b  53         c  80

11  a  145       b  306        c  1008

# Decimal fractions  tenths

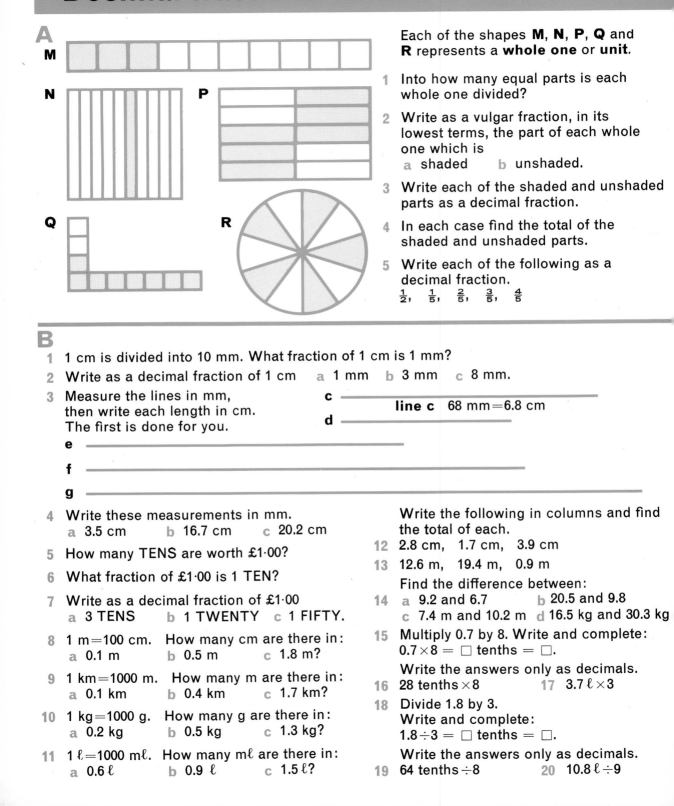

**A**

M

N

P

Q

R

Each of the shapes **M**, **N**, **P**, **Q** and **R** represents a **whole one** or **unit**.

1 Into how many equal parts is each whole one divided?

2 Write as a vulgar fraction, in its lowest terms, the part of each whole one which is
   a shaded    b unshaded.

3 Write each of the shaded and unshaded parts as a decimal fraction.

4 In each case find the total of the shaded and unshaded parts.

5 Write each of the following as a decimal fraction.
   $\frac{1}{2}$,  $\frac{1}{5}$,  $\frac{2}{5}$,  $\frac{3}{5}$,  $\frac{4}{5}$

**B**

1 1 cm is divided into 10 mm. What fraction of 1 cm is 1 mm?

2 Write as a decimal fraction of 1 cm  a 1 mm  b 3 mm  c 8 mm.

3 Measure the lines in mm, then write each length in cm. The first is done for you.

c ————————————
**line c  68 mm=6.8 cm**
d ————————

e ——————————

f ————————————

g ——————————————

4 Write these measurements in mm.
   a 3.5 cm    b 16.7 cm    c 20.2 cm

5 How many TENS are worth £1·00?

6 What fraction of £1·00 is 1 TEN?

7 Write as a decimal fraction of £1·00
   a 3 TENS    b 1 TWENTY    c 1 FIFTY.

8 1 m=100 cm.  How many cm are there in:
   a 0.1 m    b 0.5 m    c 1.8 m?

9 1 km=1000 m.  How many m are there in:
   a 0.1 km    b 0.4 km    c 1.7 km?

10 1 kg=1000 g.  How many g are there in:
   a 0.2 kg    b 0.5 kg    c 1.3 kg?

11 1 ℓ=1000 mℓ.  How many mℓ are there in:
   a 0.6 ℓ    b 0.9 ℓ    c 1.5 ℓ?

Write the following in columns and find the total of each.

12 2.8 cm,   1.7 cm,   3.9 cm

13 12.6 m,   19.4 m,   0.9 m

Find the difference between:

14 a 9.2 and 6.7        b 20.5 and 9.8
   c 7.4 m and 10.2 m  d 16.5 kg and 30.3 kg

15 Multiply 0.7 by 8. Write and complete:
   $0.7 \times 8 = \square$ tenths $= \square$.

Write the answers only as decimals.

16 28 tenths ×8        17 3.7 ℓ ×3

18 Divide 1.8 by 3.
   Write and complete:
   $1.8 \div 3 = \square$ tenths $= \square$.

Write the answers only as decimals.

19 64 tenths ÷8        20 10.8 ℓ ÷9

# Shapes   triangles and their angles

**A**  Look carefully at each angle in the triangles marked **X**, **Y** and **Z**.

A set square can be used to answer the following questions.

1  In which triangle is there an angle of 90° (a right angle)?
This triangle is a **right-angled triangle**.

2  In which triangle is each of the three angles less than 90° (an acute angle)?
This triangle is an **acute-angled triangle**.

3  In which triangle is there an angle greater than 90° (an obtuse angle)?
This triangle is an **obtuse-angled triangle**.

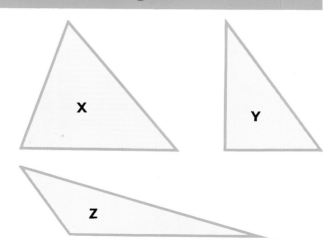

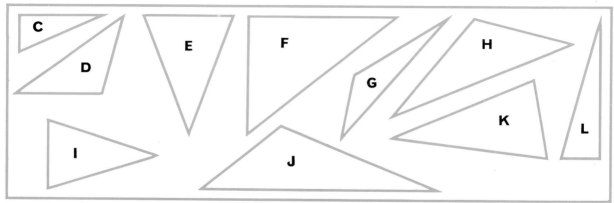

From the triangles lettered **C** to **L**, write the members of the following sets.

4  O = {obtuse-angled triangles}

5  A = {acute-angled triangles}    6  R = {right-angled triangles}

**B**

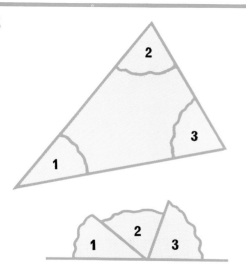

1  On a piece of gummed paper draw a large acute-angled triangle. Cut it out.

2  Mark the angles **1**, **2** and **3**, as shown in the diagram.

3  Tear off each of the angles, fit them together and stick them on a sheet of paper.

4  Now draw on gummed paper
a  a large obtuse-angled triangle
b  a large right-angled triangle.
Repeat the exercise with each triangle.
See if you get the same result each time.

5  Write and complete:
The three angles of a triangle together equal ☐ right angles or ☐°.

6  Why is it impossible to have two right angles or two obtuse angles in a triangle?

# Shapes triangles, sides and angles

Triangles are named   a  according to their angles   b  according to the lengths of their sides.

## A

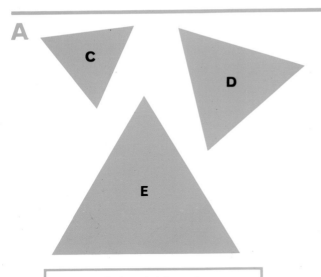

**Equilateral triangles**
3 sides of equal length
3 equal angles each of 60°
3 lines of symmetry

1  Measure in mm the sides of the triangles **C**, **D** and **E**. What do you find in each case? Triangles which have three sides of equal length are called **equilateral triangles**.

2  Get a 60° set square. Fit it into each angle. What is the size of each angle in an equilateral triangle?

3  Use a ruler and a 60° set square to draw an equilateral triangle with sides 90 mm long. Check the size of each angle, then cut out the triangle.

4  Fold the triangle in half so that one half fits exactly on the other half.
Mark the fold line with a dotted line.

5  The dotted line is a line of symmetry. Why?

6  There are two more lines of symmetry in the equilateral triangle. Find them by folding. Mark them with a dotted line.

7  Draw two more large equilateral triangles and repeat exercises **4**, **5** and **6**.

## B

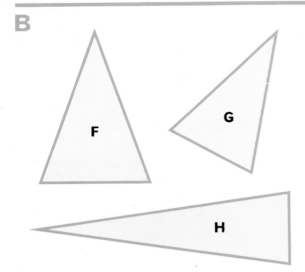

**Isosceles triangles**
2 sides of equal length
2 equal angles opposite the equal sides
1 line of symmetry

1  Measure in mm the sides of the triangles **F**, **G** and **H**. What do you find about the lengths of two sides in each triangle? Triangles which have two sides of equal length are called **isosceles triangles**. 'Isosceles' means 'equal legs'.

2  Draw an isosceles triangle with two 70 mm sides.

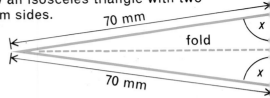

3  Cut out the triangle and fold it so that one 70 mm side fits on the other. What do you find about the angles marked $x$?

4  Mark the fold with a dotted line.
This is a line of symmetry. How do you know?

5  Test by folding if there are other lines of symmetry.

6  Draw two more isosceles triangles and repeat exercises **3**, **4** and **5**.

# Shapes   triangles, sides and angles

## A

1   Measure in mm the sides of triangle **X**.
What do you find about the lengths of the three sides?

2   Now measure in mm the lengths of the three sides of triangles **Y** and **Z**.
What do you find about the lengths of the sides in each triangle?
Triangles which have three sides of different lengths are called **scalene triangles**.
'Scalene' means 'uneven; unequal'.

3   Draw and cut out a large scalene triangle.
Tear off the angles and show by fitting that they are of different sizes.

4   Draw and cut out another large scalene triangle.
Test by folding if it has a line of symmetry.

5   Repeat exercises **3** and **4** with other scalene triangles.

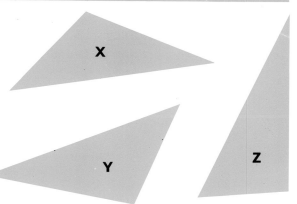

**Scalene triangles**
No equal sides
No equal angles
No line of symmetry

## B

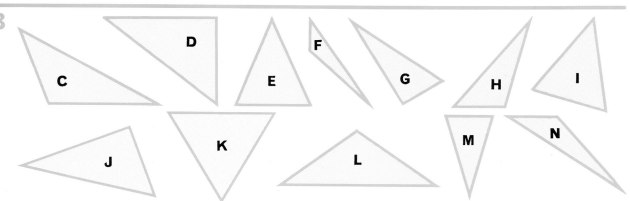

From the triangles lettered **C** to **N**, write the members of each of the following sets.
You may use a ruler and set square if you wish.

O = {obtuse-angled triangles}    I = {isosceles triangles}    R = {right-angled triangles}
A = {acute-angled triangles}    S = {scalene triangles}    E = {equilateral triangles}

## C

The height of a triangle is the length of the perpendicular drawn from the **vertex** to the base.

1   Measure in mm for triangles **S** and **T**
a   the base      b   the height.

2   Draw three large acute-angled triangles.
Use a set square to draw a perpendicular from the vertex to the base of each.

3   Measure their heights in mm.

4   Now draw three obtuse-angled triangles.
Repeat exercises **2** and **3**.

# Multiplication graded practice

First work Section **A**. Mark the answers and correct any mistakes.

Then work and correct Section **B**.

Do the same with Sections **C**, **D** and **E**. Write the answers only.

**A**
| 1 $41 \times 5$ | 2 $33 \times 3$ | 3 $60 \times 6$ | 4 $72 \times 4$ | 5 $90 \times 7$ |
| 6 $57 \times 6$ | 7 $38 \times 7$ | 8 $29 \times 8$ | 9 $64 \times 9$ | 10 $76 \times 5$ |

Write the answers to the following as £s.

| 11 $16p \times 7$ | 12 $28p \times 4$ | 13 $34p \times 3$ | 14 $52p \times 5$ | 15 $73p \times 6$ |
| 16 $29p \times 8$ | 17 $23p \times 9$ | 18 $25p \times 6$ | 19 $87p \times 2$ | 20 $36p \times 5$ |

**B**
| 1 130 $\times 5$ | 2 370 $\times 4$ | 3 590 $\times 9$ | 4 280 $\times 7$ | 5 400 $\times 6$ |
| 6 207 $\times 8$ | 7 409 $\times 7$ | 8 606 $\times 5$ | 9 803 $\times 6$ | 10 308 $\times 9$ |

**C**
| 1 354 $\times 2$ | 2 136 $\times 5$ | 3 493 $\times 4$ | 4 581 $\times 7$ | 5 268 $\times 3$ |
| 6 675 $\times 6$ | 7 936 $\times 8$ | 8 248 $\times 9$ | 9 276 $\times 7$ | 10 724 $\times 5$ |

Make sure that in each answer the point is in the correct place.

**D**
| 1 £0·06 $\times 7$ | 2 £0·03 $\times 9$ | 3 £0·07 $\times 6$ | 4 £0·36 $\times 3$ | 5 £0·41 $\times 5$ |
| 6 £0·13 $\times 8$ | 7 £0·54 $\times 4$ | 8 £0·27 $\times 7$ | 9 £0·21 $\times 9$ | 10 £0·79 $\times 3$ |

**E**
| 1 £3·00 $\times 6$ | 2 £2·40 $\times 5$ | 3 £6·30 $\times 10$ | 4 £2·63 $\times 3$ | 5 £3·76 $\times 7$ |
| 6 £4·15 $\times 4$ | 7 £2·43 $\times 9$ | 8 £5·27 $\times 6$ | 9 £1·09 $\times 8$ | 10 £6·30 $\times 5$ |

**F**

Find by the shortest method:
1 $78+78+78+78+78$
2 $39p+39p+39p+39p$
3 £1·75+£1·75+£1·75.
4 Find the number which is eight times bigger than 89.
5 What is the cost of 6 metres of cloth at £3·45 per metre?
6 The sides of a square each measure $43\frac{1}{2}$ cm. Find its perimeter in
a cm b m and cm.

7 A flask holds $3\frac{1}{2}$ litres. How many litres and millilitres will 7 flasks hold?

8 John has saved 79p.
Mary has saved twice as much as John. Find their total savings.

9 The mass of a parcel is 870 g.
Find the mass of 5 such parcels
a in g b in kg and g.

10 $\frac{58}{6)\,x}$  What is the value of $x$ in this example?

# Division graded practice

First work Section **A**. Mark the answers and correct any mistakes.
Then work and correct Section **B**.
Do the same with Sections **C, D, E, F** and **G**. Write the answers only.

**A**
1. $7\overline{)91}$
2. $5\overline{)85}$
3. $4\overline{)76}$
4. $6\overline{)96}$
5. $3\overline{)87}$
6. $5\overline{)375}$
7. $7\overline{)462}$
8. $6\overline{)390}$
9. $4\overline{)392}$
10. $9\overline{)612}$
11. $8\overline{)1168}$
12. $3\overline{)2916}$
13. $7\overline{)4151}$
14. $9\overline{)6471}$
15. $5\overline{)3825}$

**B**
1. $6\overline{)840}$
2. $9\overline{)1080}$
3. $8\overline{)2560}$
4. $5\overline{)3450}$
5. $4\overline{)4880}$
6. $7\overline{)721}$
7. $3\overline{)921}$
8. $6\overline{)654}$
9. $4\overline{)3632}$
10. $9\overline{)8136}$

> If there is a remainder, remember to show it as in the example:
> $$7\overline{)2347} = 335 \text{ rem. } 2$$

**C**
1. $643 \div 6$
2. $987 \div 4$
3. $831 \div 8$
4. $709 \div 5$
5. $745 \div 3$
6. $1235 \div 7$
7. $1307 \div 9$
8. $3113 \div 5$
9. $4514 \div 8$
10. $5167 \div 9$
11. $4387 \div 4$
12. $3509 \div 7$
13. $2007 \div 2$
14. $3916 \div 6$
15. $9103 \div 8$

**D**
1. $8\overline{)64p}$
2. $6\overline{)84p}$
3. $7\overline{)35p}$
4. $5\overline{)80p}$
5. $9\overline{)81p}$

Check the answers first. Write them as £s, making sure that
the point is in the correct place in each answer.

**E**
1. $4\overline{)£0·92}$
2. $5\overline{)£1·65}$
3. $8\overline{)£2·80}$
4. $5\overline{)£5·05}$
5. $6\overline{)£3·24}$
6. $9\overline{)£0·99}$
7. $4\overline{)£1·84}$
8. $7\overline{)£3·22}$
9. $6\overline{)£2·82}$
10. $3\overline{)£1·41}$

**F**
1. $2\overline{)£4·08}$
2. $6\overline{)£12·18}$
3. $9\overline{)£18·72}$
4. $7\overline{)£21·63}$
5. $4\overline{)£20·12}$
6. $6\overline{)£7·80}$
7. $3\overline{)£4·80}$
8. $8\overline{)£13·60}$
9. $5\overline{)£17·50}$
10. $9\overline{)£33·30}$

**G**
1. $£18·72 \div 6$
2. $£16·75 \div 5$
3. $£16·73 \div 7$
4. $£32·82 \div 3$
5. $£11·12 \div 2$
6. $£19·71 \div 9$
7. $£18·64 \div 8$
8. $£43·56 \div 4$
9. $£73·08 \div 6$
10. $£84·91 \div 7$

**H** Share these sums of money equally.
Write the remainder in pence.
1. £1·50 among 7 children
2. £10·00 among 3 children
3. £5·50 among 9 children
4. Find the value of $x$ when
   a. $7x = 952$    b. $8x = £3·60$.

5. The perimeter of a square is 114 cm.
   Find the length of one side of the square.

6. $3\frac{1}{2}$ kg of apples were put into 5 bags in
   equal quantities.
   How many g were there in each bag?

7. Share £2·60 between Joan and Peter,
   giving Joan 10p more than Peter.

# Multiplication and division

## A

1 Multiply by 10.
   a  7.6 cm    b  0.75 kg    c  0.9 cm

2 Divide by 10.
   a  £27    b  8 litres    c  3.6 m

3 Divide each of the following by 4.
   a  32 g    b  320 g    c  3.2 kg

4 Divide by 6.
   a  48 mm    b  480 mm    c  4.8 m

5 Divide by 8.
   a  56 ml    b  560 ml    c  5.6 l

Find the value of $x$ in each of the following.

6 $3 \times x = 7 \times 3$     11 $48 \div 6 = 24 \div x$
7 $x \times 8 = 8 \times 6$     12 $12 \div 4 = x \div 3$
8 $6 \times 2 = x \times 3$     13 $36 \div x = 30 \div 5$
9 $2 \times 5 = 10 \times x$     14 $x \div 9 = 40 \div 8$
10 $9 \times x = 0 \times 8$     15 $28 \div 7 = x \div 4$

## B

In each of the following, find the value of $y$.
1 $y \times 8 = 120$     2 $y \times 5 = 95p$
3 $y \times 6 = 582$     4 $y \times 4 = £3.56$

**Multiplication answers should always be checked by division.**
e.g. $46 \times 8 = 368$ check $368 \div 8 = 46$
Check these answers by division.
Correct those which are wrong.
5 $35 \times 7 = 255$     6 $83p \times 6 = £4.98$
7 $203 \times 4 = 852$     8 $£1.08 \times 9 = £9.92$

Find the value of $z$ in the following.
9 $z \div 7 = 13$     10 $z \div 9 = 37$
11 $z \div 5 = 18$ rem. 4    12 $z \div 8 = £1.34$

**Division answers should always be checked by multiplication.**
e.g. $236 \div 4 = 59$ check $59 \times 4 = 236$
Check these answers by multiplication.
Correct those which are wrong.
13 $294 \div 7 = 42$
14 $£3.68 \div 8 = £0.46$ or $46p$
15 $1535 \div 5 = 37$
16 $£18.63 \div 9 = £2.70$
17 $627 \div 6 = 104$ rem. 5
18 $£7.25 \div 4 = £1.82$ rem. 1p

## C

1 Mother bought 3 ices at 12p each. How much change did she receive from 2 TWENTIES?
2 Find the change from £1 after paying for five bus fares at 9p each.
3 John saved a FIVE each day during the months of May and June. Find his total savings.
4 A pack of 8 ball-point pens cost £3.12. What is the cost in pence of one pen?
5 1 metre of ribbon costs 70p. Find the cost of   a  50 cm    b  10 cm.
6 A leg of lamb weighing 3 kg costs £5.40. Find the price:
  a  per kg    b  per 500 g    c  per 100 g.
7 9 tins of fruit salad cost £3.06. What is the cost of   a  1 tin    b  5 tins?
8 £4.60 is paid for 10 litres of oil. What is paid for   a  1 litre    b  7 litres?
9 A cup costs 27p and a saucer 15p. Find the cost of   a  a cup and a saucer   b  6 cups and 6 saucers.
10 A maths set costs £1.60 and a writing-pad costs 39p. What is the total cost of 4 of each?

11
  £0.37
  £0.37
  £0.37
  £0.37
  £0.37
  £0.37
  £0.37
  £0.37

Mother bought some jars of jam in the supermarket. She received this bill.
  a  How many jars of jam did she buy?
  b  What was the price per jar?
  c  Find in the shortest way the total cost of the jam.

Find the cost of these purchases.
12 7 tins of baked beans @ 13p per tin
13 250 ml of cream @ 76p per ½ l
14 6 lemons @ 2 for 15p
15 800 g of cheese @ 60p per ½ kg
16 200 g of plaice @ 90p per ½ kg
Mark and correct the answers **12** to **16**.
17 Name the coins, using as few as possible, to pay for each bill.

# Capacity litres and millilitres

**A**

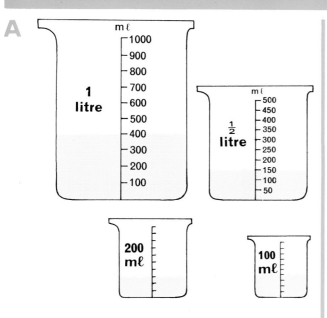

The measures shown above are used to find the capacity of containers.

Capacity is the amount a container holds, measured in litres $\ell$ and millilitres $m\ell$.

1 Look at the scale marked on the 1 litre measure. How many $m\ell$ are represented by each division?

2 How many $m\ell$ are represented by each division on the scale of:
   a the $\frac{1}{2}\ell$ measure
   b the 200 $m\ell$ measure
   c the 100 $m\ell$ measure?

3 Read from the scale how many $m\ell$ of liquid are shown in each measure.

4 Get a set of capacity measures.
   Look at the scale marked on each measure and find out how many $m\ell$ are represented by each division.

5 Collect several containers of different sizes and shapes, e.g. pans, bowls, jars, bottles, etc.
   Estimate, according to size, the capacity of each   a to the nearest $\frac{1}{2}$ litre
   or   b to the nearest 100 $m\ell$.

6 Check your estimates, using the most convenient measure.

7 Draw a table and keep a record of your estimates and measurements.

**B**

| 1 litre($\ell$) = 1000 millilitres ($m\ell$) |
|---|

By how many $m\ell$ are the following less than 1 litre?

1 a 600 $m\ell$     b 300 $m\ell$     c 750 $m\ell$
2 a 800 $m\ell$     b 150 $m\ell$     c 540 $m\ell$

By how many $m\ell$ are these measures greater or less than $\frac{1}{2}$ litre?

3 a 900 $m\ell$     b 350 $m\ell$     c 590 $m\ell$
4 a 425 $m\ell$     b 830 $m\ell$     c 180 $m\ell$

Find how many $m\ell$ there are in:

5 a $\frac{1}{4}\ell$     b $\frac{3}{4}\ell$     c $\frac{1}{10}\ell$
6 a $\frac{1}{5}\ell$     b 1 $\ell$ 600 $m\ell$     c 3 $\ell$ 450 $m\ell$.

Change these measures to $\ell$ and $m\ell$.

7 a 1200 $m\ell$     b 3100 $m\ell$     c 5250 $m\ell$
8 a 4300 $m\ell$     b 2750 $m\ell$     c 7050 $m\ell$

Another way of writing $\ell$ and $m\ell$ is to **separate them by a point** and write the answers as $\ell$.
e.g. 2450 $m\ell$ = 2 $\ell$ 450 $m\ell$ = 2.450 $\ell$

Draw these tables and complete.

|   | $\ell$ | $m\ell$ |   | litres |
|---|---|---|---|---|
| 9  1250 $m\ell$ = | | | = | |
| 10  3700 $m\ell$ = | | | = | |
| 11  2050 $m\ell$ = | | | = | |
| 12  5010 $m\ell$ = | | | = | |
| 13  305 $m\ell$ = | | | = | |
| 14  4750 $m\ell$ = | | | = | |

Change the following to $m\ell$.

15 a 1.500 $\ell$     b 3.850 $\ell$     c 2.070 $\ell$
16 a 8·750 $\ell$     b 0.370 $\ell$     c 10.6 $\ell$

Write to the nearest $\ell$.

17 a 5 $\ell$ 950 $m\ell$     b 4 $\ell$ 350 $m\ell$
18 a 9 $\ell$ 850 $m\ell$     b 10 $\ell$ 480 $m\ell$
19 a 7.500 $\ell$     b 19.650 $\ell$

Write to the nearest $\frac{1}{2}\ell$.

20 a 3 $\ell$ 100 $m\ell$     b 6 $\ell$ 450 $m\ell$
21 a 9 $\ell$ 200 $m\ell$     b 9 $\ell$ 920 $m\ell$
22 a 8.330 $\ell$     b 15.780 $\ell$

# Capacity   litres and millilitres

**A**

W 1 ℓ 500 mℓ   X 960 mℓ   Y 1.590 ℓ   Z 750 mℓ

1 Which of the containers holds
   a the most   b the least?

2 By how many mℓ is
   a the capacity of **W** greater than that of **X**
   b the capacity of **Z** less than that of **Y**?

3 The jar **W** was filled 5 times with water
   which was then poured into a 10-litre
   cask.
   a Find in ℓ the total amount of water.
   b How much more will the cask hold?

4 Find the capacity in mℓ of a container
   a ½ that of **W**
   b ¼ that of **X**   c ⅓ that of **Z**.

5 Find in ℓ and mℓ the total capacity of
   the four containers **W, X, Y** and **Z**.

**B**

1 Get a jar which holds more than 1 litre.
   Weigh it in g as accurately as possible.

2 Pour in 1 ℓ of water and weigh it again.

3 Find the mass of 1 ℓ of water.
   Make this record.

| | grams |
|---|---|
| Mass of jar filled with 1 ℓ of water | |
| Less mass of empty jar | _____ |
| Mass of 1 ℓ of water | _____ |

If the answer is between 950 g and
1050 g, the measuring and weighing have
been well done.

> **Remember  1 litre (1000 mℓ) of water
> weighs 1 kg (1000 g).**

4 What is the mass of ½ ℓ of water?
   Check your answer by weighing.

5 Write the mass of:
   a 1 mℓ   b 100 mℓ   c 200 mℓ of water.

6 Write in kg the mass of water in each of
   the full containers **W, X, Y** and **Z** above.

**C** Find the missing measure in each of the
   following.

1 640 mℓ + ☐ mℓ = 1 litre
2 270 mℓ + ☐ mℓ = ½ litre
3 ☐ mℓ + 950 mℓ = 1.5 litres
4 ½ litre − ☐ mℓ = 450 mℓ
5 2 litres − ☐ mℓ = 1020 mℓ
6 0.8 litres − ☐ mℓ = 150 mℓ

Find the cost of:
7 100 mℓ if 1 litre costs £1·10
8 200 mℓ if ½ litre costs 45p
9 1 litre if 200 mℓ costs 24p
10 1½ litres if ¼ litre costs 16p.

11 A cup holds 250 mℓ. How many cupfuls
   can be poured from 2½ ℓ?

12 In a 3-litre jug, there are 870 mℓ of water.
   How many ℓ and mℓ are needed to fill it?

13 How many litres of squash will fill
   4 bottles each holding 650 mℓ?

14 3.600 ℓ × 6
   Write the answer to the nearest litre.

15 A medicine spoon holds 5 mℓ.
   If a girl takes one spoonful of medicine
   four times daily, for how long will a bottle
   holding 300 mℓ last?

16 Find the mass of water in kg which is
   put into jars holding:
   a 3500 mℓ   b 2¼ ℓ   c 1 ℓ 400 mℓ.

17 A bucket holds 10 ℓ of water. Find the
   mass of the water in kg if it is ¾ full.

18 A 60-litre barrel when empty weighs 8 kg.
   Find its mass when full of water.

19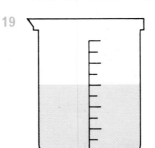
   The measuring jug
   holds 1 litre.
   a What fraction of
   1 ℓ of liquid
   has been put into
   the jug?
   b If ½ ℓ is poured
   out, what fraction
   of 1 ℓ remains?

# 24-hour clock

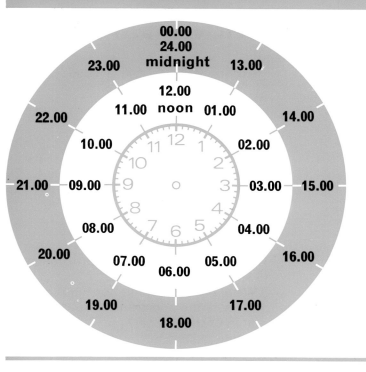

Bus, railway, ship and airline timetables use the **24-hour clock** to state the times of arrival and departure of journeys.

**Remember**
The 24-hour clock numbers the hours from 00 to 24, that is, for a whole day from **midnight** to **midnight**.

When writing 24-hour clock times, a.m. and p.m. are never used.

All 24-hour clock times are written with four figures, the first two for hours, the last two for minutes past the hour.

A point usually separates the hours from the minutes, e.g.
4.20 a.m. is written 04.20
4.20 p.m. is written 16.20.

Study the diagram above, it will help you to find the following answers.

**A** Change these a.m. times to 24-hour clock times.

1  2.00 a.m.
2  7.00 a.m.
3  10.00 a.m.
4  5.10 a.m.
5  11.05 a.m.

6  half past 4
7  quarter to 8
8  25 min past 9
9  10 min to 12
10  18 min past 12

Change these p.m. times to 24-hour clock times.

11  3.00 p.m.
12  8.00 p.m.
13  11.00 p.m.
14  4.20 p.m.
15  6.15 p.m.

16  5 min past 10
17  25 min to 6
18  4 min past 7
19  5 min to 9
20  6 min to 12

Change these 24-hour clock times to 12-hour clock times. Write a.m. or p.m.

21  02.05
22  14.30
23  08.55
24  13.20
25  17.40

26  19.50
27  10.44
28  22.35
29  06.02
30  00.07

**B** Find the number of minutes to the next hour from:

1  03.10
2  07.45
3  10.50

4  01.23
5  09.34
6  13.17

7  00.06
8  12.51
9  23.33.

10  Write each of the above times to the nearest hour.

How many minutes are there from:

11  06.15 to 06.50
12  19.08 to 19.35
13  07.12 to 07.40
14  02.50 to 03.25

15  10.35 to 11.15
16  14.28 to 15.12
17  17.45 to 18.09

How many hours and minutes are there from:

19  11.45 to 12.50
20  16.20 to 17.46
21  07.52 to 09.00

22  05.25 to 06.40
23  13.38 to 16.00
24  22.45 to 00.15?

18  23.08 to 00.05?

# 24-hour clock timetables

## A

| Flight No. | BZ 61 | BZ 62 | BZ 63 | AL 4 | AL 6 |
|---|---|---|---|---|---|
| Birmingham dep. | 08.55 | 10.30 | 14.45 | 15.50 | 18.45 |
| Dublin arr. | 09.40 | 11.15 | 15.30 | 16.40 | 19.35 |

The table gives the times of five flights from Birmingham to Dublin.

1 Find the places on a map. Name the sea over which the aircraft flies.

2 Write in words the 12-hour clock departure times of flights
BZ 62    AL 4    AL 6.

3 Write in figures the 12-hour clock arrival times in Dublin of flights
BZ 61    BZ 63.

4 Find the time taken for each flight in minutes.

5 A traveller missed flight BZ 61 by 10 min.
a Write the 24-hour clock time for the next flight.
b How long did he have to wait?
c By how many h and min was his arrival in Dublin delayed?

6 The distance 'as the crow flies' from Birmingham to Dublin is approximately 315 km.
a Write the time in min for flight BZ 61.
b What is the approximate speed in km/h of the aircraft?

## B

### Passenger and Car Ferry Service
### London to Jersey (Channel Islands) via Weymouth

| London dep. | Weymouth Quay arr. | Weymouth Quay dep. | Jersey arr. |
|---|---|---|---|
| 09.30 | 12.15 | 13.30 | 20.45 |

1 Find London, Weymouth and Jersey on a map. Follow the route of the journey.

2 Name the sea across which the ferry service travels.

3 Write in 12-hour clock time, the time of
a departure from London
b arrival in Jersey.

4 Find the time in h and min for the journey.

5 Write in 12-hour clock time in words, the
a arrival time at Weymouth Quay
b departure time from Weymouth Quay.

6 Find the time in h and min for the journey
from a London to Weymouth Quay
b Weymouth Quay to Jersey.

7 What is the waiting time in h and min at Weymouth?

## C

The times of three trains from King's Cross to Bradford are given in the timetable.

| King's Cross | 07.50 | 09.10 | 11.25 |
|---|---|---|---|
| Wakefield | 10.17 | 11.51 | 13.39 |
| Bradford | 11.16 | 12.52 | 14.32 |

1 Find the time taken for each of the journeys from King's Cross to Bradford.

2 Which is    a the fastest    b the slowest journey?

Find these times. 3    depart King's Cross 07.50    arrive Wakefield ☐
4    depart Wakefield 11.51    arrive Bradford ☐
5    depart King's Cross 11.25    arrive Wakefield ☐

6 Find the time taken for each of these journeys.

# Graphs

**A** The graph shows the number of children in each of the classes in the school.

Without counting the squares in the columns, answer questions **1** to **5**.

1 How many classes are there in the school?

2 In which class is there
   a the largest number of children
   b the smallest number of children?

3 Write the classes in order of size, the smallest first.

4 In which class are there fewer than 20 children?

5 In which classes are there more than 30 children?

6 Look again at the graph and find what is shown
   a on the vertical axis
   b on the horizontal axis.

7 How many children are represented by one division on the vertical scale?

8 How many children are there in each of the classes 1, 2, 3, 4 and 5?

9 Look carefully at the columns which represent classes 6 and 7.
   Notice that a half division is used.
   How many children are there in each of these classes?

10 Find the total number of children in the school.

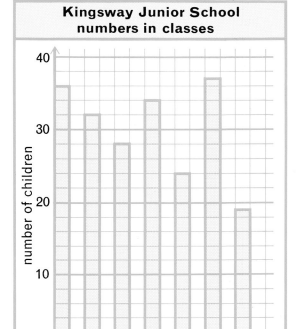

**Kingsway Junior School numbers in classes**

11 If all the children were arranged in seven classes of equal numbers, how many would there be in each class?
   This number is called the average.

12 Which of the classes are
   a above the average
   b below the average in size?

---

**B Oakwood Junior School: class numbers**

| classes | 1 | 2 | 3 | 4 | 5 | 6 |
|---------|---|---|---|---|---|---|
| girls | 19 | 15 | 9 | 18 | 8 | 13 |
| boys | 14 | 12 | 13 | 17 | 9 | 15 |

1 Make a list of the classes and write the total number of children in each.

2 On 5 mm squared paper, draw a graph to show the number of children in each class.
   Mark the horizontal and vertical axes, as in the example above.

3 How many classes are there in the school?

4 Find the total number of children.

5 If all the children were arranged in classes of equal numbers, how many would there be in each class?

6 Write and complete:
   The class average is ☐ children.

7 Draw a dotted line across the graph to show the average.

8 Which classes are
   a below the average
   b above the average?

9 Find the average of 25, 18, 16, 32 and 29.

# Graphs

**A** The graph shows the amounts of money collected by each class in the school for the Children's Aid Fund.

Answer questions **1** to **7** by looking at the graph.

1 What is shown on the horizontal axis?
 How many classes are there in the school?

2 Name the axis on which the money is shown.

3 How much money is represented on the scale by
 a one division    b a half division?

4 Write the class numbers in order, putting first the class which collected the most money.

5 Find the difference between the greatest and smallest amounts.

6 Which class collected twice as much as class 1?

7 Which class collected one third as much as class 4?

8 Draw this table and complete it by reading from the graph the amount of money collected by each class.

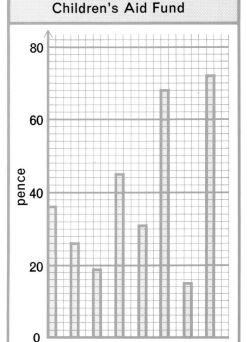

**Oakwood Junior School**
Children's Aid Fund

| class 1 | class 2 | class 3 | class 4 | class 5 | class 6 | class 7 | class 8 |
|---|---|---|---|---|---|---|---|
|  |  |  |  |  |  |  |  |

9 Find the total amount of money collected at the school.

10 What is the average amount per class?

11 Which classes collected
 a more than the average    b less than the average?

---

**B** The table gives the amount of money collected by each class in the Abbey Junior School.

| class 1 | class 2 | class 3 | class 4 | class 5 | class 6 | class 7 | class 8 | class 9 | class 10 |
|---|---|---|---|---|---|---|---|---|---|
| 40p | 60p | 37p | 56p | 52p | 46p | 42p | 51p | 33p | 43p |

1 Write the class numbers in order, putting first the class which collected the most.

2 What is the smallest amount of money collected by a class?

3 On 2 mm graph paper draw a graph to show the money collected by each class.
 a On the horizontal axis mark the class numbers.
 b Mark pence on the vertical axis. The scale can start at 30p. Give a reason for this.

4 Now draw the graph showing the amounts of money.

5 From the table, find the total amount of money collected at the school.

6 Find the average per class. Check this answer.

7 Draw a dotted line across the graph and mark it 'average'.

8 Which classes collected
 a more than the average
 b less than the average?

9 What do you notice about class 6?

# Shapes   perimeters and areas

**A**

> **Remember**
> The **perimeter** of a shape is
> the distance all round it.

The perimeter is a **length** which is
measured in **length units**,
e.g. **mm, cm, m**.

1  Find by measuring in mm the perimeter
of the shapes **W, X, Y** and **Z**.
Check the measurements.

2  Write each perimeter
a  in cm and mm      b  in cm only.

3  Write the name of shape **W**, shape **X**,
shape **Y** and shape **Z**.

4  Estimate which of the shapes has the
largest surface (area).

5  Writing letters only, put the shapes in
order, the largest area first.

6  Move the palm of your hand over the surface of the top of your desk,
the blackboard, the front of a cupboard, the top of the teacher's table.
Which has      a  the largest      b  the smallest area?

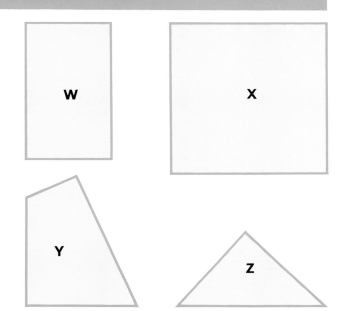

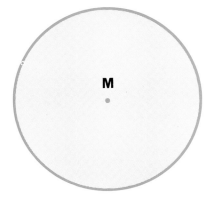

**B**

1  Measure in mm the sides of shape **C**.

2  What is the name of this shape?

3  Find its perimeter      a  in mm      b  in cm.

4  Draw the shape using a set square.
Cut it out and colour its surface.

5  Now draw two more squares, **D** and **E**, with sides
measuring 4 cm and 35 mm, respectively.
Cut them out and colour the surfaces.

6  Fit the three squares one over the other and find which
has the largest area.

7  Measure in mm the radius of the circle.

8  Draw and carefully cut out circle **M**. Colour it.

9  Draw three more circles, **N, O** and **P**, making the radius
5 mm bigger each time.

10  Cut out these circles and colour their surfaces.

11  Fit the circles one over the other and find which has
a  the largest      b  the smallest area.
Notice that the areas of squares or circles can be
compared by fitting one over the other.

12  Look again at the shapes in Section **A**. Can you
compare their areas by fitting one over the other?

# Shapes   measuring surfaces ; areas

**A**

Shapes **E, F, G** and **H** are rectangles. The surface of each has been covered with squares of equal size.

1 Which rectangle has
   a the smallest surface      b the largest surface?
   How do you know?

2 Which of rectangles **E, F, G** and **H** have surfaces of the same size? How do you know?

3 On squared paper, draw a rectangle with the same number of squares as **E** but arranged in a different way.
   Now do the same with **F, G** and **H**.

4 On squared paper draw rectangles which have surfaces:
   a half the size of **G**      b half the size of **E**
   c twice the size of **H**      d one-third the size of **F**.

**B**

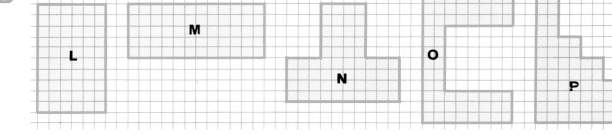

The surfaces of each of the different shapes are covered exactly by squares of equal size.

1 Count the number of squares which cover
   a the rectangle **L**      b the rectangle **M**.

2 What do you discover about their areas?

3 Now count the squares which cover the shapes **N, O** and **P**.

4 What do you discover about their areas?

5 On a sheet of squared paper, draw four different shapes each of which has the same area.

6 On squared paper draw:
   a a square      b a rectangle
   c three other shapes each having an area of 100 squares.

> **Remember**   Shapes which are different can have the same area.

**C**   Squares of the same size have been used to measure area.

1 Look at these shapes. Which of them fit together to cover a surface?

**equilateral triangles**          **hexagons**          **circles**

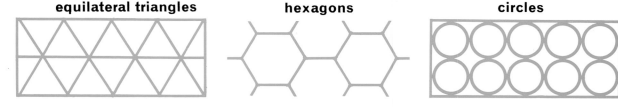

2 Give a reason why, for measuring surfaces:
   a circles could not be used      b squares are the most suitable shape.

# Shapes measuring surfaces; areas

**A**

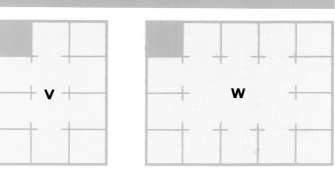

1 Measure in cm the length and width of the shapes **V, W** and **X**.

2 What is the name of each shape?

3 Find the perimeter of shape **V**, shape **W**, shape **X**. Give the unit of measurement.

4 The shapes can be covered by **square centimetres (cm²)**. What is the length of each side of a square centimetre?

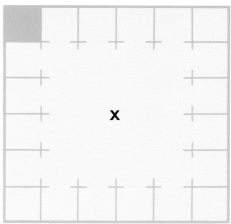

5 How many square centimetres will cover each shape? Write and complete:
area of shape **V** = ☐ cm²
area of shape **W** = ☐ cm²
area of shape **X** = ☐ cm².

6 On cm squared paper draw two shapes each of which is different from shape **V** but has the same area.

7 Find the perimeter of each shape. In each case, the area remains the same but the perimeter changes in length.

8 Repeat the exercise with shapes **W** and **X**.

9 Find
  a the perimeter
  b the area of shapes **Y** and **Z**.

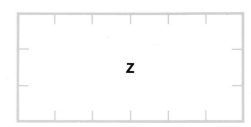

**B** Find the area in cm² of each of the shapes **M, N** and **O**.

1

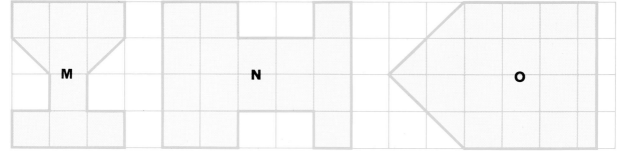

On cm squared paper draw:

2 a square equal in area to shape **M**; shape **N**    3 a rectangle equal in area to shape **O**.

# Shapes measuring surfaces; areas

A  The drawing **X** is an irregular shape, the
surface of which is covered with square
centimetres.

To find its **approximate** area:

count the whole squares

count the part squares which are a
**half** or **more**.
These are marked with a dot and are
counted as whole squares.

The part squares which are less than
half are not counted.

1  Now find in cm² the approximate area of
the shape.

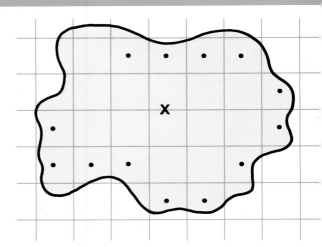

B

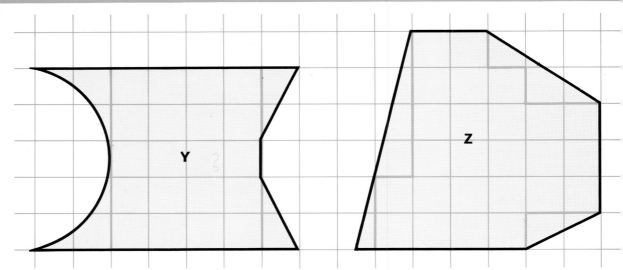

The drawings **Y** and **Z** are irregular
shapes which are covered with square
centimetres.

The whole squares have been enclosed
within the coloured lines to make
counting easier.

1  Count the whole squares in shape **Y**.
How many are there?

2  Count the part squares which are a half
or more.
How many are there?

3  Find the approximate area.

Write and complete:
The approximate area of shape **Y** is ☐ cm².

4  Find the approximate area of shape **Z**.

5  Which of the shapes **X, Y** and **Z** has
a  the greatest area
b  the smallest area?

6  On a sheet of cm squared paper, draw an
irregular shape and find its approximate
area.

7  Compare the surfaces of different kinds
of large leaves by drawing round their
edges and then finding their approximate
areas.

# Distance time and speed

**A**

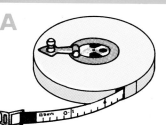

Get a 10-metre tape. Examine it carefully. Find the metre and $\frac{1}{2}$ metre markings. What other units are shown on the tape?

Learn how to use the tape correctly, then practise with a partner measuring distances
a to the nearest m     b in m and cm.

1 Measure and mark a distance of 50 m.
2 With a partner using a stop-watch, find how many seconds it takes
a to walk 50 m     b to run 50 m.
3 Draw and complete this table.

| distance | time taken to | | | |
|---|---|---|---|---|
| | walk | | run | |
| 50 m | | s | | s |
| 100 m | | s | | s |
| 250 m | | s | | s |
| $\frac{1}{2}$ km | min | s | min | s |

A kilometre is the unit for measuring long distances.

| **1 kilometre (km) = 1000 metres (m)** |
|---|

4 How many m in:
a $\frac{1}{4}$ km   b $\frac{3}{4}$ km   c $\frac{1}{10}$ km   d $\frac{1}{100}$ km?

A boy scout found he could
walk 1 km in 10 min; run 1 km in 5 min; cycle 1 km in 4 min.
At these speeds how far can he:
5 walk in     a 30 min     b 1 h
6 run in     a 30 min     b 1 h
7 cycle in     a 30 min     b 1 h?

Speed is usually given in km per hour (km/h).
Write in km/h a speed of:
8 20 km in 15 min     9 8 km in 10 min
10 $\frac{1}{2}$ km in 1 min     11 136 km in 20 min.

How many km are travelled:
12 in $\frac{1}{4}$ h at a speed of 72 km/h
13 in 45 min at a speed of 80 km/h
14 in 10 min at a speed of 12 km/h?

**B**

1 A motor car travels at 60 km/h.
At this speed how far will it travel in:
a 1 min     b 10 min     c $\frac{3}{4}$ h?

2 A truck travelled 90 km in 1 h 30 min.
a How many km did it travel in 30 min?
b Write the speed of the truck in km/h.

3 Give a reason why the following statement is not true.
"A runner sprints 100 m in 10 seconds, therefore he can run 1000 m (1 km) in 100 seconds (1 min 40 s)."

4 An aeroplane flies 3300 km in 5 h.
a Find its speed in km/h.
b How many km does it fly in 1 min?

The table gives the distances in km of some towns from London on the A1 route to Edinburgh.

| From London to | |
|---|---|
| Stamford | 121 km |
| Grantham | 185 km |
| Doncaster | 256 km |
| Darlington | 385 km |
| Newcastle | 438 km |
| Edinburgh | 630 km |

Find the distance:
5 from Stamford to Darlington
6 from Grantham to Doncaster
7 from Doncaster to Newcastle.
8 Find the distance of each town from Edinburgh.

9 A motorist estimated that it would take 4 hours approximately to drive from Doncaster to London by the A1.
Find his average speed in km/h.

10 Find to the nearest km his average speed to complete the journey in approximately 3 h.

11 Find the distance from Grantham to Darlington.

12 Find the time taken for this journey at an average speed of 80 km/h.

13 At an average speed of 70 km/h, how long would the journey from London to Edinburgh take?

# Shapes circles

## A

Practise using a pair of compasses.
Copy these patterns making them much larger.
Make up some patterns of your own design.

1

2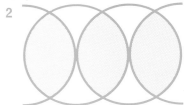

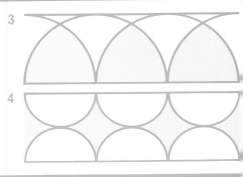

3

4

## B

M

centre

radius   26 mm

N

centre

diameter 36 mm

O

centre

P

centre

1   The measurements of the
    circles **M** and **N** are given.
    With a pair of compasses draw
    circles of the same sizes.

2   Cut out the circles and check
    that you have drawn them
    correctly by fitting them on the
    drawings.

3   Measure circles **O** and **P** and
    then draw them the same sizes.

4   Cut them out and fit them on
    the drawings. See if they are
    correctly drawn.

5   Draw circles of these radii.
    a 25 mm   b 40 mm   c 58 mm

6   Write the diameter of each of
    these circles. Check your
    answers by measuring.

7   Find the radius of each of these
    circles, the diameter of which is:
    a 60 mm   b 90 mm   c 72 mm.

8   Draw these circles.

## C

1   a   Draw a circle with a radius of 30 mm.
    b   Draw any six radii of this circle and
        measure them.
        What do you find about their lengths?

2   Repeat this exercise many times, using
    circles of different radii.
    What do you find each time?

3   a   Draw a circle with a diameter of 70 mm.
    b   Draw any six diameters of this circle
        and measure them.
        What do you find about their lengths?

4   Repeat this exercise many times using
    circles with different diameters.
    What do you find each time?

5   How many   a radii   b diameters
    do you think you can draw in any circle?

**Remember** In the same circle
    all **radii** are equal in length
    all **diameters** are equal in length
    a diameter is twice the length of the radius
    a radius is half the length of the diameter.

# Shapes circles, measuring diameters

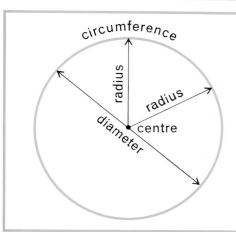

## Circles

Words to remember

The **circumference** is the distance round the edge of a circle or its perimeter.

The **radius** is the distance from the centre of the circle to its circumference.

The **diameter** is the distance across a circle from the circumference to the circumference through the centre.

To draw circles of given size with a pair of compasses either the **diameter** or the **radius** must be known.

The diagram shows a method of measuring the diameter of circular objects.

A FIVE is used in the example.

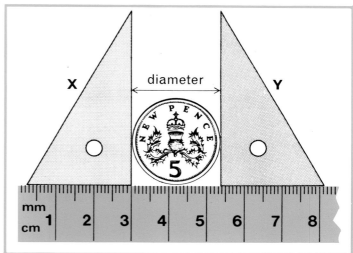

1 Place set square **X** along the ruler in line with a centimetre mark.

2 Place the FIVE so that its edge touches the set square and the ruler.

3 Move set square **Y** along the ruler to the edge of the FIVE.

4 From the ruler read the length of the diameter in mm.

5 Write and complete:
The diameter of a FIVE is ☐ mm.

6 What is the radius of a circle of this size?

7 In the same way, find the diameter of each of these coins in mm.
a  a TEN    b  a TWO    c  a penny

8 Draw this table.
List the coins you have measured.
Enter the diameter and the radius of each.

| object | diameter | radius |
|--------|----------|--------|
| a FIVE<br>a TEN<br>etc. | | |

Enter the following measurements in the table.

9 Collect a number of circular objects, e.g. cups, plates, tin lids, buttons, jars. Measure in mm the diameter of each.

10 Find the diameter to the nearest cm of
a  the top of a bucket
b  the bottom of the same bucket.

11 Measure to the nearest cm the diameter of a cycle wheel.

12 Use a pair of compasses to draw circles of these measurements.
radius      50 mm;   35 mm;   19 mm
diameter   90 mm;   68 mm;   52 mm

# Shapes  circles, measuring circumferences

**A**

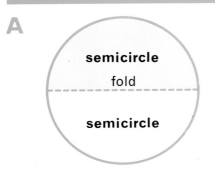

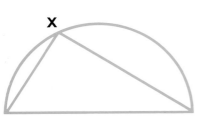

1 Draw and cut out a circle of 50 mm diameter.
2 Fold it in half. The fold line is a line of symmetry. Give the reason.
3 How many lines of symmetry can be drawn in a circle?
4 Cut the circle into two equal parts. Each part is called a **semicircle**. ('semi' means 'half'.)
5 a Draw a semicircle of 40 mm diameter.
  b Mark any point **X** on the circumference and join it by two lines to the ends of the diameter as shown.
6 Measure with a set square the angle at **X** on the circumference. Name the shape drawn in the semicircle.
7 Draw another semicircle of radius 25 mm.
  Repeat exercises **5b** and **6**.
  What do you discover about the angle at the circumference?
8 Draw six other semicircles each of different diameters. Repeat exercises **5b** and **6**. You should get the same results.

**B**

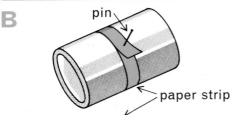

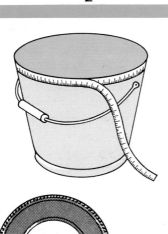

The following are different ways of **measuring the circumference** of circular objects.

**Method 1**
a Get a circular tin, a cylinder.
b Wrap a paper strip around the tin taking care to keep it level.
c Stick a pin through both pieces of the strip where they overlap.
d Lay the strip flat and measure in mm the distance between the pin-holes.

**Method 2**
a Get a bucket and a tape-measure marked in cm.
b Wrap the tape-measure round the top rim holding the end firmly in place.
c Read the measurement of the circumference to the nearest cm.
d In the same way, measure the circumference of the bottom rim of the bucket.

**Method 3**
a Get a motor tyre or a cycle wheel.
b Make a mark on the tyre and on the floor, as shown in the diagram.
c Roll the tyre forward along a straight line until it has turned round once. Mark the floor again.
d Measure to the nearest cm the distance between the two marks, which is the circumference of the tyre.

Collect a number of circular objects of different sizes.
Choose the most suitable method to measure the circumference of each.

# Decimal fractions tenths and hundredths

**A** | **A reminder** Decimal fractions are based on the **tens number system**.

Look back to page 49, Section **A**.

| Th | H | T | U | t tenths | |
|----|---|---|---|----------|---|
| 1 | 1 | 1 | 1 | 1 | 1 |

decreases 10 times for each place →

In the diagram above, the figure 1 in the **tenths** column is moved one place to the **right**.
Its value is 10 times smaller than **one tenth** ($\frac{1}{10}$).
You now have to find the value of
**one tenth of one tenth** or $\frac{1}{10}$ **of** $\frac{1}{10}$.

Look at this diagram.

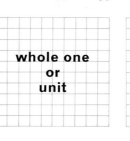

1 How many strips like that marked **x** are there in the whole one or unit?

2 What fraction of the whole one is one strip?

3 How many small squares like that marked **y** are there in each strip?

4 What fraction of a strip is one small square?

5 Without counting, how many small squares are there in the whole one?

6 What fraction of the whole one is one small square?
Write: $\frac{1}{10}$ of $\frac{1}{10} = \frac{1}{100} = 0.01$.

7 How many hundredths of the whole ones marked **R, S** and **T** are shaded?

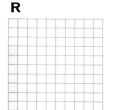 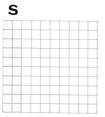 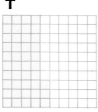

**R**       **S**       **T**

Write the answers first as vulgar fractions then as decimal fractions.

**B** | 0.07 is read as 'nought point nought seven'.
0.43 is read as 'nought point four three'.
Read the numbers to a partner who can check from the answer book.

1 a 0.71    b 0.03    c 0.15
2 a 0.91    b 0.06    c 0.88

Write as decimal fractions:

3 4 hundredths      4 9 hundredths
5 23 hundredths     6 58 hundredths
7 71 hundredths     8 95 hundredths.

Write and complete the following.

9 $0.17 = \frac{\square}{10} + \frac{\square}{100} = \frac{\square}{100}$
10 $0.32 = \frac{\square}{10} + \frac{\square}{100} = \frac{\square}{100}$
11 $0.68 = \frac{\square}{10} + \frac{\square}{100} = \frac{\square}{100}$
12 $0.45 = \frac{\square}{10} + \frac{\square}{100} = \frac{\square}{100}$

**C**

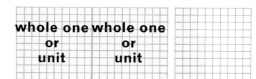

The shaded part shows 2 units and 36 hundredths or 2.36.
2.36 is read as 'two point three six'.

Write and complete:

1 2.36 = □ tenths □ hundredths
2 5.04 = □ hundredths
3 7.68 = □ tenths □ hundredths
4 10.05 = □ tenths □ hundredths
5 20.28 = □ hundredths.

Write these answers as decimals.

6 $\frac{7}{10} + \frac{4}{100}$      7 $\frac{2}{10} + \frac{8}{100}$
8 $1 + \frac{4}{10} + \frac{7}{100}$    9 $9 + \frac{6}{10} + \frac{1}{100}$
10 $12 + \frac{57}{100}$      11 $27 + \frac{3}{100}$

Write the numbers shown on each abacus picture as a decimal.

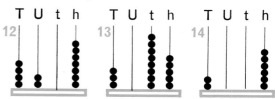

12    T U t h     13    T U t h     14    T U t h

# Decimal fractions tenths and hundredths

## A

> **Remember**
> The figure in the **first place** after the decimal point is the number of **tenths**.
> The figure in the **second place** after the decimal point is the number of **hundredths**.

Write as decimals.

1 92 tenths      5 104 hundredths
2 206 tenths      6 2005 hundredths
3 76 hundredths      7 1070 hundredths
4 8 hundredths      8 3019 hundredths

Write the value of the figure underlined in each of these numbers.

9   a 7.0<u>8</u>    b 5<u>6</u>.62    c <u>3</u>2.94
10 a 3<u>3</u>.53    b 60<u>8</u>0    c 40.<u>1</u>3
11 a <u>2</u>069    b 8.<u>5</u>7    c 126.8<u>9</u>

Put these in order, the smallest first.

12 0.06,   6.0,    0.6,    60
13 1.3,    13,    0.13,    130
14 0.5,    1.25,    0.05,    1.5

Write the numbers below in columns and then find the total of each column.
Keep the decimal points in line.

15 19.8,   3.73,   1.07,   10.25
16 0.19,   0.03,   0.86,   0.47
17 27.4,   38.09,   15.02,   20.5

Find the difference between:

18 a 7 and 0.04      b 13.2 and 9.84
19 a 10.7 and 15.03    b 16.02 and 25.

Multiply each of these numbers by 100.

20 a 0.63    b 3.02    c 0.2

Make each of these 100 times smaller.

21 a 700    b 497    c 605
22 a 39    b 90    c 8

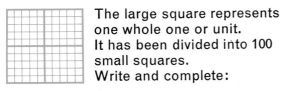

The large square represents one whole one or unit.
It has been divided into 100 small squares.
Write and complete:

23 a $\frac{1}{2} = \frac{\square}{100}$    b $\frac{1}{4} = \frac{\square}{100}$    c $\frac{3}{4} = \frac{\square}{100}$.
24 Write as decimal fractions. $\frac{1}{2}$,   $\frac{1}{4}$,   $\frac{3}{4}$.

## B

The British money system, like that of most other countries, is based on the **tens number system**, so it is called a **decimal currency**.

Previously sums of money have been written using a **pennies point** to separate the £s from the pence.

You can now think of the **pennies point** as a **decimal point**.

1 TEN is $\frac{1}{10}$ of £1·00 and is written as £0·1 or £0·10.

1 penny is $\frac{1}{100}$ of £1·00 written as £0·01.

1 Write as decimals of £1·00
   a a TWO    b a FIVE.

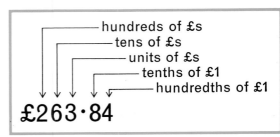

Study the diagram.

Write the value in money of each of the figures underlined.

2 a £2·<u>8</u>9    b £0·<u>7</u>5    c £<u>2</u>08·61
3 a £8·<u>4</u>0    b £18·0<u>7</u>    c £<u>5</u>9·92

Write as £s, using a decimal point.

4 a 4 TENS    b 9 TENS    c 21 TENS
5 a 7p    b 46p    c 208p
6 £58 and 72 pence
7 £20, 4 TENS and 3p

### Metres and centimetres

8 1 m is divided into 100 cm. What decimal fraction of 1 m is   a 10 cm   b 1 cm?

Write these measurements as metres.

9 a 7 cm    b 14 cm    c 55 cm
10 a 136 cm    b 270 cm    c 408 cm

11 How many cm in:
   a 0.09 m   b 4.32 m   c 16.5 m   d 9.76 m?

# Number, Money and Measures problems

**A**

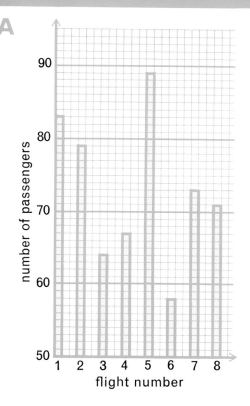

The graph shows the number of passengers on each of certain British Airways daily flights.

1 How many flights were there?
Name the axis on which they are shown.

2 What is shown on the vertical axis?

3 What does one division on this axis represent?

4 Draw this table. Complete it by reading the number of passengers from the graph.

| flight | 1 | 2 | 3 | 4 | 5 | 6 | 7 | 8 |
|---|---|---|---|---|---|---|---|---|
| passengers | | | | | | | | |

5 Check the answers and correct any mistakes.

6 Look at the numbers of passengers. Give a reason why the scale on the vertical axis begins at 50.

7 Find
   a  the total number of passengers
   b  the average number of passengers for each flight.

8 If each aircraft seats 94 passengers, find
   a  the greatest number which could travel on these flights during the day
   b  the total number of empty seats.

9 If the single fare for a flight is £30, how much money was paid altogether?

10 If all the seats were taken, how much would be paid?

---

**B** On the dashboard of a motor car there is an instrument called an **odometer** which measures the distance travelled in **kilometres** and **tenths of a kilometre**.

The tenths are often shown in a different colour.

| 0 | 1 | 3 | 6 | 8 | 2 |
|---|---|---|---|---|---|

The drawing shows the dial of an odometer. The reading is 1368.2 km.

What will be the reading when the car has travelled:

1 another 10 km

2 another 100 km   3 another 1000 km?

How far must the car travel for:

4 the 2 to change to 3

5 the 8 to change to 9

6 the 6 to change to 7

7 the 3 to change to 4?

**X** | 0 | 8 | 1 | 0 | 0 | 4 |
|---|---|---|---|---|---|---|

**Y** | 1 | 3 | 4 | 2 | 2 | 6 |
|---|---|---|---|---|---|---|

**Z** | 1 | 3 | 7 | 0 | 1 | 3 |
|---|---|---|---|---|---|---|

8 Write the odometer readings on the dials **X**, **Y** and **Z**.

9 The reading on dial **X** was taken after a journey of 93.7 km. What was the reading at the start of the journey?

10 What will be the reading on dial **X** when the car has travelled a further 308.6 km?

11 How many more km must the car travel for the reading on the dial **X** to be 10 000 km?

12 The reading on dial **Y** was at the start of a journey. The reading on dial **Z** was at the end. Find the length of the journey.

# Number, Money and Measures problems

**A** Bills given in supermarkets should always be checked. **T** stands for 'total'.

| X | | Y | | Z | |
|---|---|---|---|---|---|
| | £0·17 | | £0·37 | | £0·39 |
| | £0·36 | | £0·37 | | £0·07 |
| | £0·73 | | £0·37 | | £0·54 |
| | £0·06 | | £0·37 | | £0·28 |
| | £0·05 | | £0·37 | | £0·12 |
| **T** | £1·37 | **T** | £1·85 | **T** | £1·30 |

1 Which of the totals of bills **X**, **Y** and **Z** is not correct?

2 By how much is this bill incorrect?

3 Find the correct total of the three bills together. Check the answer.

4 Write the least number of coins required to pay the total of the three bills.

Stores and shops have sales, when prices are reduced.

| SPRING SALE | 5p in the £ off all prices |
|---|---|

5 By how much will these prices be reduced?

  a £5·00  b £12·00  c £20·00  d £1·20

6 What will be the sale prices?

7 By what fraction of £1 is each article reduced?

| Fares | 5p | 6p | 8p | 10p |
|---|---|---|---|---|
| Friday | 39 | 18 | 25 | 57 |
| Saturday | 24 | 32 | 10 | 41 |
| Sunday | 46 | 20 | 7 | 19 |

The table gives the number of passengers who travelled on a bus on each of the three days and also the fares they paid.

8 How many people travelled each day?

9 How many paid each fare, 5p, 6p, 8p and 10p? Check the answers.

10 Find the total sum of money taken for each of the fares.

**B**

1 Find the mass of the water in a barrel which holds 40 litres.

2 The water in a can has a mass of 20.5 kg. Write in $\ell$ and m$\ell$ the capacity of the can.

3 Susan saves a TWO every day during April, May and June for her holiday. How much does she save altogether?

4 How many packets of tea each containing 200 g can be made from 5.600 kg?

5

  a How much water must be added to $\frac{1}{2}$ $\ell$ of squash?

  b What is the total amount of the squash and water?

  c How many $\frac{1}{4}$ $\ell$ glasses can be filled from the diluted squash?

6 A car uses 1 litre of petrol to travel 8 km. The petrol tank when full holds 60 litres. How many km will the car travel on a full tank?

7 A packet of 200 sheets of paper weighed $2\frac{1}{2}$ kg. Find in g the mass of
  a 100 sheets  b 20 sheets  c 60 sheets.

Mother buys material to make 10 curtains each 1 m 70 cm long.

8 Write the length of one curtain in m.

9 At £3·50 per m, what is the cost?

10 Find in m the length of material she buys.

11 The mass of three parcels is 3 kg 700 g, 2 kg 400 g and 5 kg, respectively.

Find  a their total mass
      b the average mass of the parcels.

12

| Hours of Business | |
|---|---|
| Monday, Tuesday, Wednesday | $\begin{cases} 8.30–12.30 \\ 2.00–5.00 \end{cases}$ |
| Thursday | 8.30–1.00 |
| Friday | 9.00–6.30 |

For how many hours is the office open?

# Fixing position

**A**

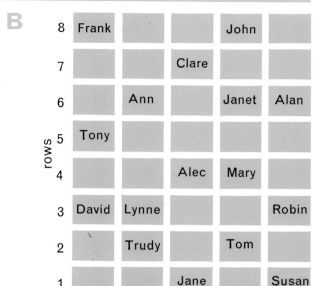

| | red | yellow | blue | green |
|---|---|---|---|---|
| 5 | Tom | Charles | Roy | Gordon |
| 4 | John | Tony | Paul | Robert |
| 3 | Peter | Alec | George | Frank |
| 2 | David | Philip | Dennis | Jack |
| 1 | Terry | James | Alan | Stephen |

rows / columns

The diagram shows the names of the boys in a P.E. class, arranged in teams each with a different colour.

1 How many teams are there?
2 Name the team colours.
3 How many boys are there
  a in each team    b in the class?
4 Write the names of the boys
  a in the blue team
  b in the fourth row.
5 Name the boy who is in the blue team on the fifth row.
6 Now name the boys in these positions.
  a green team, 2nd row
  b red team, 1st row
  c yellow team, 3rd row
7 For the following examples, letters only are given for the colours.
The letter for the team colour is written before the number of the row.
Name the boys in these positions.
  a G,4    b B,1    c Y,4
  d Y,2    e R,3    f G,3
8 Write the position of each of these boys.
  a Terry    b George    c Stephen
  d Charles    e Dennis    f John

**B**

| | A | B | C | D | E |
|---|---|---|---|---|---|
| 8 | Frank | | | John | |
| 7 | | | Clare | | |
| 6 | | Ann | | Janet | Alan |
| 5 | Tony | | | | |
| 4 | | | Alec | Mary | |
| 3 | David | Lynne | | | Robin |
| 2 | | Trudy | | Tom | |
| 1 | | | Jane | | Susan |

rows / columns

The plan shows how a block of seats was set out in columns and rows for the school concert.

1 How many columns of seats were there?
2 How many rows of seats were there?
3 How many seats were there altogether in the block?
4 Each seat was given a letter for the column and a number for the row.
For example, Ann's seat was B,6.
Find her seat on the plan.
5 Name the child whose seat was D,2.
Write the letter and the number of the seat of each of these children.
6 Alan    7 Alec    8 Janet
9 Tony    10 Lynne    11 Trudy
12 Name the child whose seat was
  a E,3    b C,7    c A,3.
Find the letter and the number of the seat for:
13 Helen who sat between Ann and Janet
14 Phillip who sat behind Alan
15 Sally who sat in front of Mary
16 Richard who sat next to David and Lynne.

# Fixing position

**A**

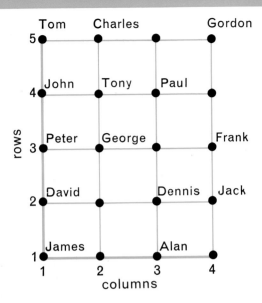

**B**

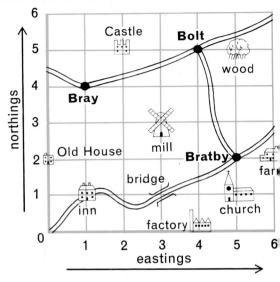

The diagram shows the P.E. positions of a class of boys standing in four teams. Some of the boys' names are omitted.

Notice that, in the diagram above, instead of the spaces, the **lines** have been numbered across and up.

The position of Paul is 3,4, that is 3 across and 4 up.

The position of Gordon is 4,5, that is 4 across and 5 up.

The number across is always written first.

Name the boys in these positions.

1  1,5           2  4,2           3  3,1
4  3,2           5  2,4           6  4,3

Write the positions of:

7   John          8   Charles        9   Peter
10  George        11  James          12  David.

On a piece of cm squared paper, draw the plan of a class arranged in 8 columns and 6 rows. Show each of these positions by a dot.

13  4,6           14  3,5           15  2,4
16  7,2           17  8,1           18  6,6

To fix the positions of places, the map is divided into a network of cm squares which is called a **grid**.

The numbers across the horizontal line at the bottom starting from 0 are called **eastings**.

The numbers along the vertical line at the side starting from 0 are called **northings**.

Write the positions of:

1  the village of Bray       7   the inn
2  the Old House             8   the mill
3  the Castle                9   the church
4  the factory              10   the village of Bolt
5  the village of Bratby    11   the farm
6  the bridge               12   the wood.

13  There is a sand-pit which is not marked on the map at 0,5. Name the nearest village to the sand-pit.

What is the direction from:

14  the inn to the wood
15  the Castle to the village of Bray
16  the church to the factory
17  the point 5,3 to Bratby?
18  The map is drawn to the scale 1 cm to 1 km.

What is the shortest distance from
a  the inn to Bray   b  Bolt to the factory?

# Circles arcs

**A**

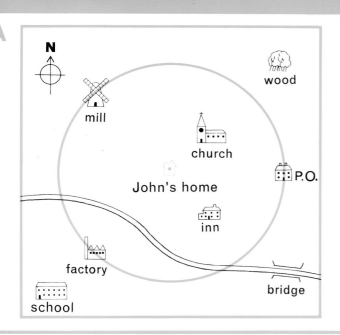

The map shows the positions of some places which are near to John's home.

The map is drawn to a scale 30 mm to 1 km.

To find which places are 1 km from his home, he draws a circle as shown.

1 At which point does he make the centre of the circle?

2 What is the radius of the circle?

3 Which of the places are 1 km from John's home?

4 Which places are   a less than 1 km   b more than 1 km from his home? How do you know?

5 Get a map of the district around your school. Draw a circle to the correct scale. Then find some places which are approximately 1 km from the school.

---

**B**

1 Measure in mm the length of a radius of the circle.

2 **C, D, E, F, G** are any points on the circumference. What is the length in mm of the lines **OC, OD, OE, OF** and **OG**? How do you know?

> **Remember**   All points on the circumference of a circle are of equal distance from its centre.

3 a Draw a circle of 35 mm radius.
   b Mark any six points on its circumference.
   c What is the distance from the centre to each of the points?
Check your answer by measuring.
**CD** is a part of the circumference.
It is called an **arc**.

4 Name by letters four other arcs of the circle.

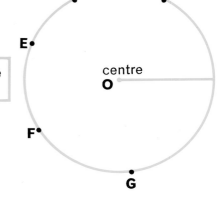

---

**C**

1 In the diagram, **MN** is part of the circumference of a circle. It is an arc of the circle.
Measure in mm the length of the radius of the arc.

2 Measure in mm the length of the radius of the arcs **OP, QR,** and **ST**.

# Circles arcs

**A** In the diagram two circles with centres at **O** and **P** are drawn.

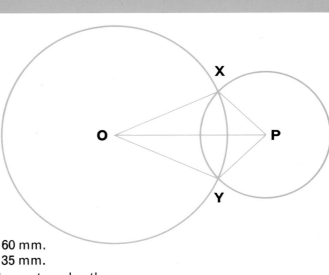

1 Measure in mm the distance between the two centres.

2 Measure in mm:
  a the radius of the circle with centre **O**
  b the radius of the circle with centre **P**.

3 Name by letter the points at which the circles cut each other.

4 Write in mm the length of the lines
  a **OX** and **OY**    b **PX** and **PY**.
  Check your answers by measuring.

5 Draw a line **AB** 80 mm long.
  a With **A** as centre, draw a circle of radius 60 mm.
  b With **B** as centre, draw a circle of radius 35 mm.

6 Mark the points **X** and **Y** at which the circles cut each other.
  Write in mm the lengths of the lines    a **AX** and **AY**    b **BX** and **BY**.

---

**B**

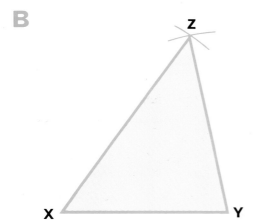

In this diagram, instead of drawing two circles, arcs only have been made.

1 Measure the line **XZ**. What is the radius of the arc which has its centre at **X**?

2 Measure the line **YZ**. What is the radius of the arc which has its centre at **Y**?

3 What is the name of the shape drawn?

4 What is the length of each side   **XY   YZ   XZ**?

5 There is another shape you can draw which is exactly the same as the one shown, but in a different position. Draw it.

6 Draw a line 60 mm long and call it **XY**. On this line draw a triangle **XYZ** with the other two sides respectively 55 mm and 35 mm long.

---

**C** **Fixing a point**

Captain Flint, the pirate, buried his treasure on a desert island in the South Seas. He left behind in his old sea-chest a parchment on which he had written the instructions for finding the treasure.

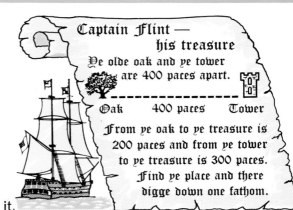

Captain Flint —
                his treasure
Ye olde oak and ye tower
are 400 paces apart.
- - - - - - - - - - - - - - -
Oak      400 paces      Tower

From ye oak to ye treasure is
200 paces and from ye tower
to ye treasure is 300 paces.
Find ye place and there
digge down one fathom.

1 Make a diagram to a scale of 20 mm to 100 paces to show how the position of the buried treasure could be found.

2 In how many places must the treasure seekers dig?

3 A fathom is a special measure. Find out about it.

# Measuring temperature

**A**

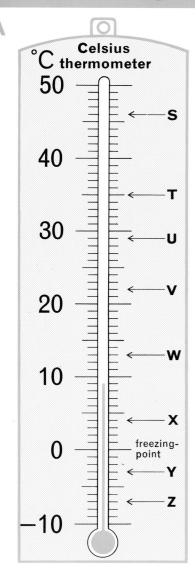

°C Celsius thermometer

50
— S
40
— T
30
— U
20
— V
10
— W
— X
0    freezing-point
— Y
— Z
−10

Get a Celsius thermometer like the one shown in the picture. There may be one hanging in the class-room.

This thermometer is used to measure the hotness or coldness of the air.

The hotness or coldness of the air is called its **temperature**.

Look at the thermometer. It consists of a sealed glass tube partly filled with a liquid, usually mercury or alcohol.

1 Place your finger on the bulb at the bottom of the tube. Watch the level of the liquid in the tube. Describe what happens.

2 Take your finger away. What happens now to the level of the liquid?

3 Put the thermometer in a warm, sunny place and again watch what happens to the level of the liquid.

4 Put the thermometer in a cool, shady place. What happens to the level of the liquid?

You have seen that the level of the liquid in the thermometer moves in two directions:

It rises as the temperature goes up.

It falls as the temperature goes down.

As the temperatures rise and fall, they are measured on the marked scale alongside the tube.

The **unit of measurement** of temperature is called a **degree Celsius** which is written as **°C**.

The weather man on TV or Radio gives in his forecast the probable temperature in °C.

Listen to him and check his forecast by reading a thermometer.

**B** Look at the scale on the thermometer shown above.

1 How many degrees Celsius does one small division represent?

2 What is the highest temperature which can be measured on this thermometer?

3 Read the temperature shown by the liquid in the tube.

4 What would be the temperature if it
 a rose by 9°C   b fell by 7°C?

The freezing-point marked 0° on the scale is the temperature of the air when water turns to ice.

5 How many degrees below freezing-point can be measured on this scale?

6 Write this temperature. Remember a minus sign (−) shows temperatures below freezing-point.

7 Find a reason why mercury or alcohol is used in the tube instead of water.

# Measuring temperature

**A** Look again at the picture of the Celsius thermometer on the previous page.

1 Name by letters the points marked on the scale which are above freezing-point (0°C).

2 From freezing-point count up the number of degrees to **S**.
Write the temperature at **S**.

3 In the same way, find and write the temperature at each of the points **T** to **X**.

4 By how many degrees has the temperature fallen from:
a **S** to **V**     b **U** to **W**     c **T** to **X**?

5 From freezing-point (0° or zero) count down the number of degrees to **Z**.
Write the temperature at **Z**.
Remember the minus sign (−).

6 In the same way, find and write the temperature at **Y**.

7 By how many degrees has the temperature risen from:
a **Z** to **Y**     b **Z** to **W**     c **Y** to **X**?

The **diagram** below shows the highest and lowest Celsius temperature on each of five days.

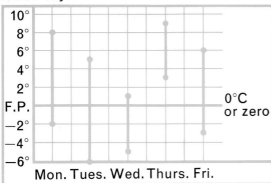

8 Draw this table and fill in the temperatures.

|  | Mon. | Tues. | Wed. | Thurs. | Fri. |
|---|---|---|---|---|---|
| highest |  |  |  |  |  |
| lowest |  |  |  |  |  |
| difference |  |  |  |  |  |

9 On which of the days would you expect to find ice on the water-tub in the garden?

**B** Get a Celsius thermometer and read the air temperature in the class-room.

1 Measure the temperature of the air in
a a corridor     b the school assembly hall

2 Which of the temperatures is the higher?

3 Find the outside temperature in
a a sunny place     b a shady place.

4 What is the difference?

5 Draw this table and keep a record of the outside temperatures at 9 a.m., noon and 3.30 p.m. every day for a week.

|  | Mon. | Tues. | Wed. | Thurs. | Fri. |
|---|---|---|---|---|---|
| 9 a.m. | °C |  |  |  |  |
| noon |  |  |  |  |  |
| 3.30 p.m. |  |  |  |  |  |

**C** A boy took the outside air temperature at noon every day. He then drew this graph.

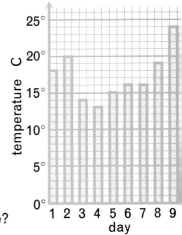

1 On how many days were the temperatures taken?

2 On which day was the temperature
a the highest
b the lowest?

3 From which day to the next was there the greatest rise in temperature?

4 Draw and fill in this table.

| day | 1 | 2 | 3 | 4 | 5 | 6 | 7 | 8 | 9 | 10 |
|---|---|---|---|---|---|---|---|---|---|---|
| temperature |  |  |  |  |  |  |  |  |  |  |

Check and correct any mistakes.

5 Add the temperatures and divide the total by 10 (the number of readings). What is the average temperature for the 10 days?

# Area   squares and rectangles

**A**  The areas of shapes have been found previously by counting centimetre squares.

You must now discover the rule for finding the **areas of squares and rectangles**.

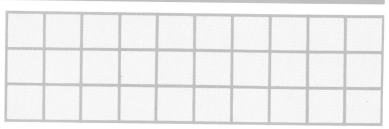

1  Measure in cm   a  the length
   b  the width or breadth of the rectangle.

2  Find in cm its perimeter.

> **Remember** The perimeter is a **length** and is measured in **length units**, mm, cm, etc.

The surface of the rectangle is covered with square centimetres (cm²).

3  How many cm² are there in the top row?

4  How many rows are there?

5  How many cm² cover the rectangle?
   Write and complete:
   Area of rectangle 10 cm long
   and 3 cm wide = (10×3) cm² = ☐ cm².

6  On cm squared paper, draw a rectangle 10 cm long and 5 cm wide.
   Find its perimeter in cm.

7  Write and complete:
   There are ☐ cm² in a row and there are ☐ rows.

8  Write and complete:
   Area of rectangle 10 cm long
   and 5 cm wide = (10×5) cm² = ☐ cm².

Complete the following.

9  Area of rectangle 10 cm long
   and 8 cm wide = (☐×☐) cm² = ☐ cm².

10  Area of square of 10 cm side
    = (☐×☐) cm² = ☐ cm².

11  Area of rectangle 9 cm long
    and 7 cm wide = (☐×☐) cm² = ☐ cm².

12  Area of square of 8 cm side
    = (☐×☐) cm² = ☐ cm².

13  Area of rectangle 7 cm long
    and 6 cm wide = (☐×☐) cm² = ☐ cm².

Find the perimeter, giving the unit of measurement for:

14  the squares in questions **10** and **12**

15  the rectangles in questions **9, 11** and **13**.

Find   a  the perimeter   b  the area
of the square or rectangle which measures:

16  7 cm long and 4 cm wide

17  length 8 cm, breadth 5 cm

18  9 cm long by 8 cm wide

19  sides of 7 cm

20  sides of 9 cm.

---

**B**  The drawings of these rectangles have been reduced to ½ size (scale 5 mm to 1 cm, 1:2).

The actual measurements are given.

Find   a  the perimeter
       b  the area of each rectangle.

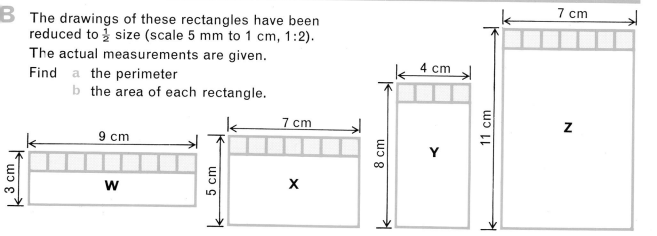

# Area   squares and rectangles

**A** Rectangles do not always have sides which measure exactly in cm.

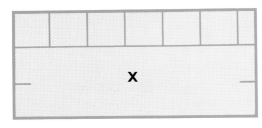

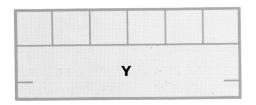

1 Measure the length of the rectangle **X** in mm. Write this length as cm.

2 Find the width of the rectangle in cm.

3 How many cm² are there in the top row?

4 How many rows are there?

5 Write and complete:
Area of rectangle **X** = (□ × □) cm² = □ cm².

6 Find the perimeter of the rectangle in cm.

7 Measure the length of rectangle **Y** in cm.

8 What is its width    a in mm    b in cm?

9 How many cm² are there in the top row?

10 How many rows are there?

11 Write and complete:
Area of rectangle **Y** = (□ × □) cm² = □ cm².

12 Find the perimeter of the rectangle in cm.

---

**B** Find   a the perimeter   b the area of each of these rectangles.

1 a sheet of paper $10\frac{1}{2}$ cm by 7 cm

2 the bottom of a box 7 cm by $5\frac{1}{4}$ cm

3 a sheet of glass, length 13 cm, breadth 5.5 cm

4 a book cover 18.5 cm by 10 cm

5 a door panel 20 cm by 16.5 cm

6 a piece of wood 50 cm by $2\frac{1}{2}$ cm

7 a card 10 cm long and 8.4 cm wide

8 a lid 85 mm by 70 mm (work in cm and cm²)

---

**C** **Square metres**

When length and width measurements of large surfaces are made in **metres**, areas are measured in **square metres (m²)**.

1 Get a metre ruler, a large set square and a stick of chalk.

2 On the floor draw a square metre. Move the palm of your hand over it and feel how much space it covers.

3 Find how many
a sheets of writing paper
b single sheets of newspaper
can be fitted into 1 m².

4 Name two surfaces which you estimate are approximately 1 m² each.

5 Estimate which of the following have an area   a more than 1 m²   b less than 1 m²
the top of a desk
the top of the teacher's table
the class-room door
the class-room window

Find the area in m² of :

6 a room 5 m long and 3 m wide

7 a carpet 4 m square

8 a wooden board 7 m by $\frac{1}{2}$ m

9 a corridor floor 26 m by 2.5 m

10 a lawn measuring 12 m by 9 m

11 a plot of ground 40 m long and 15 m wide

12 a garden 28 m by 14 m.

---

**Area of rectangles   Remember**
Area = number of units in the length × number of units in the breadth.
This is written in short as:    Area = length × breadth    or A = l × b.
The units of length and breadth must be the same.

# **Plans** drawing to scale

**A** Plans show the shape of things looked at from above.

To draw plans of large objects on small sheets of paper it is necessary to show them reduced in size by drawing them to scale.

Look at the picture of a box with a lid.
1 Write the length of the box
   a in cm     b in mm.
2 Write the width of the box
   a in cm     b in mm.
3 Use a ruler and set square to draw full size a plan of the top of the box.
4 Now draw three more plans. Make the measurements
   a $\frac{1}{2}$ size    b $\frac{1}{5}$ size    c $\frac{1}{10}$ size.

A plan can be drawn larger than the actual object.
5 Draw a plan of the box making the measurements twice the actual size.

Notice that the plans drawn get smaller or larger but the shapes remain the same.

**B**

plan of box top

The measurements on the plan of the top of a box have been drawn $\frac{1}{4}$ of the actual size.
1 Measure the length and width of the plan
   a in cm     b in mm.
2 Find the actual length and width of the box     a in cm     b in mm.
3 Write and complete:
   The plan is drawn to the scale
   1 cm to ☐ cm.
4 a If the measurements on the plan had been drawn $\frac{1}{10}$ of the actual size, find the length and width of the box.
   b To what scale had this plan been drawn? Write and complete: 1 cm to ☐ cm.

**C** The pictures drawn to a scale of 1 mm to 5 mm are from a catalogue of 'minitoys'.

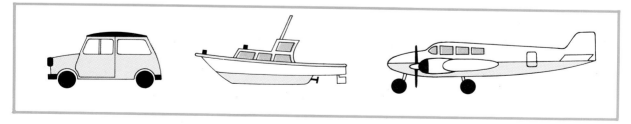

1 Measure in mm the length of     a the car     b the speedboat     c the aeroplane.
2 Find the actual length of each toy. Write the measurements     a in mm     b in cm.
3 What fraction of the actual length is each picture?
4 What fractions of the actual lengths are lines drawn to the following scales?
   a 1 cm to 4 cm     b 1 cm to 10 cm     c 1 mm to 20 mm     d 1 mm to 50 mm

# Plans drawing to scale

**A** Write the actual measurements represented by these lines.

1 _____
2 _____
3 _____
4 _____
5 _____
6 _____

**Scale**

| | |
|---|---|
| 1 cm to 5 cm | 1:5 |
| 1 cm to 100 cm (1m) | 1:100 |
| 1 mm to 10 mm (1 cm) | 1:10 |
| 1 mm to 20 mm (2 cm) | 1:20 |
| 1 mm to 100 mm (10 cm) | 1:100 |
| 1 mm to 1000 mm (1m) | 1:1000 |

Using the scale:

7 1 cm to 50 cm ($\frac{1}{2}$ m) draw lines to represent
  a 350 cm    b 4 m 50 cm    c 8.5 m

8 1 cm to 200 cm (2 m) draw lines to represent
  a 4 m    b 10 m    c 7 m

9 1 mm to 50 mm (5 cm) draw lines to represent
  a 500 mm    b 150 cm    c 350 cm

10 1 mm to 1000 mm (1 m) draw lines to represent
  a 10 m    b 45 m    c 74 m.

11 Using the symbol : write the scales given in examples 7 to 10.

The height of the boy is drawn to scale. His actual height is 150 cm.

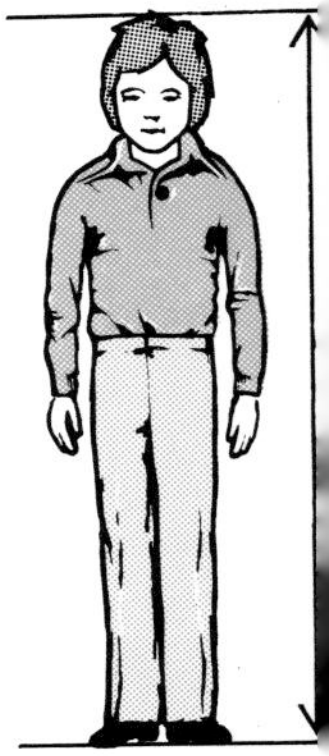

12 Measure in cm his height in the picture.

13 Write and complete:
☐ cm represents 150 cm, 1 cm represents ☐ cm.

14 Write in two ways the scale used in drawing the picture.

15 Draw lines to the same scale to show heights of:
  a 210 cm    b 165 cm    c 315 cm.

**B** Draw a plan of each of these objects to the given scale. The actual measurements are shown.

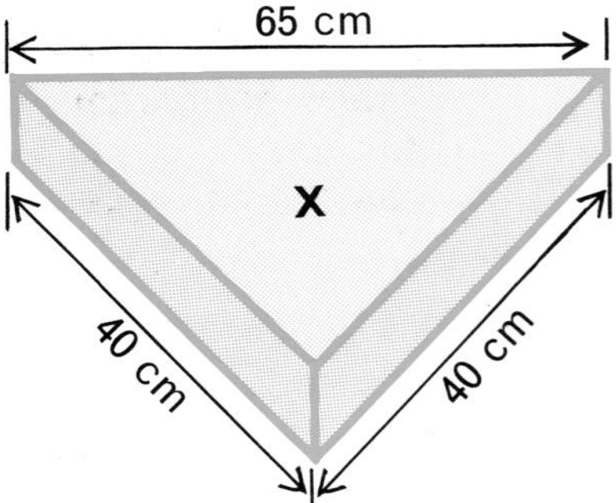

65 cm
X
40 cm 40 cm
Scale 1 cm to 10 cm (1:10)

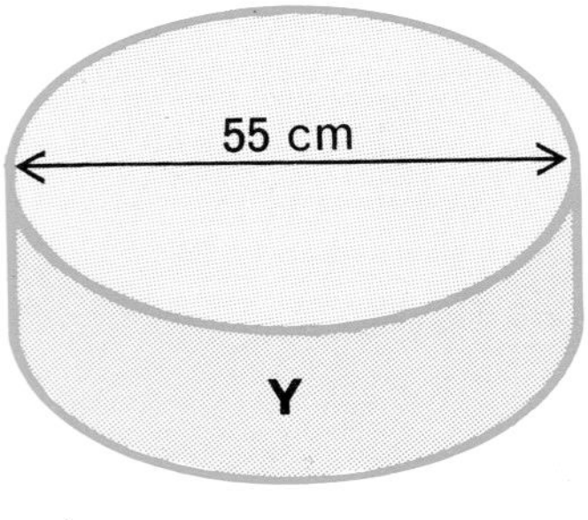

55 cm
Y
Scale 1 cm to 5 cm (1:5)

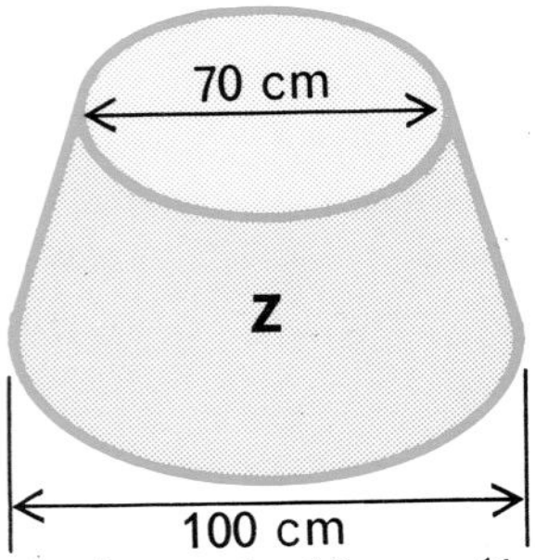

70 cm
Z
100 cm
Scale 1 mm to 10 mm (1:10)

**C**

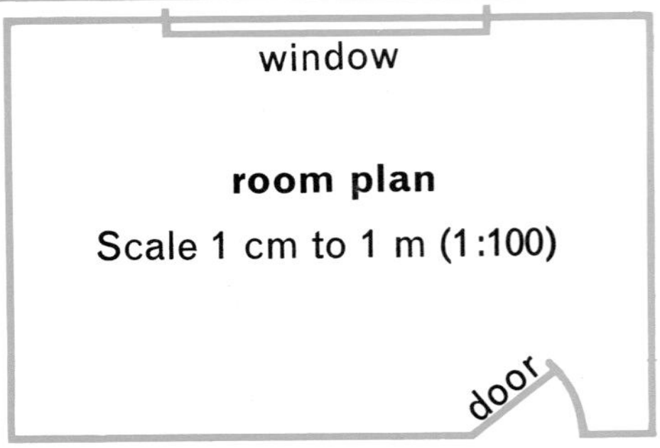

window
**room plan**
Scale 1 cm to 1 m (1:100)
door

1 This plan of a room is drawn to a given scale.
Write it as   a 1 cm to ☐ cm   b ☐ mm to 1 m.

2 What actual length in metres is represented on the plan by   a 1 mm   b 5 mm   c 15 mm?

3 Find by measuring the plan the actual measurements
of   a the length and width of the room
  b the length of the window
  c the width of the door.

4 Check the answers, then find the area of the room in m².

# Plans drawing to scale

**A**

This is a plan of a new garden which a man will make at the back of his house.

1 The plan is drawn to a scale of 1 mm to 200 mm (1:200). Write and complete:

On the plan ☐ mm represents 1 metre on the garden

☐ mm represents 2 metres on the garden.

2 How many mm represent    a   5 m    b   9 m?

3 Draw this table.

|  | plan measurements | | actual measurements | |
|---|---|---|---|---|
|  | length in mm | width in mm | length in m | width in m |
| whole garden vegetable garden lawn rose bed flower border |  |  |  |  |

4 On the plan, measure in mm the length and width of the whole garden. Write the measurements in the table.

5 Find the actual length and width of the whole garden in m. Enter these measurements in the table.

6 In the same way, complete the table for each part of the garden. Check all the measurements from the answer book.

7 Find in m² the area of:
a the whole garden
b the vegetable garden
c the rose bed.

8 Find in m the perimeter of:
a the whole garden
b the lawn
c the flower border.

**B** The tracing from a map shows the positions of five towns.

1 Write the scale of the map 10 mm to ☐ km or 1 mm to ☐ km.

2 Find the distance in km from:
a Ripton to Bingley
b Tuxley to Corley
c Linton to Ripton.

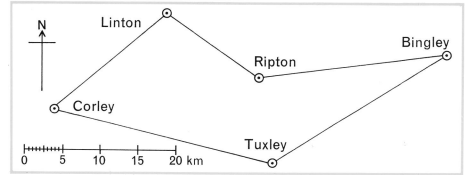

3 Find the distance and the direction from:
a Linton to Corley   b Tuxley to Bingley.

4 What is the distance in km 'as the crow flies' from Corley to Bingley?

5 Find the distance in km from Corley to Bingley:
a via Linton and Ripton   b via Tuxley.

6 Which is the shorter journey?

# Drawing triangles

## A Drawing triangles with sides of given lengths

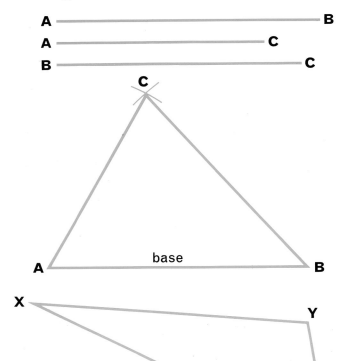

1 The sides of the triangles to be drawn are **AB, AC** and **BC**. Measure their lengths in mm.

2 Draw a line equal in length to **AB**. This line will be the base of the triangle.

3 Open the compasses to a length equal to **AC**. With **A** as centre, draw an arc.

4 Open the compasses to a length equal to **BC**. With **B** as centre, draw an arc.

5 Draw lines from **A** and **B** to the point **C** where the arcs cut each other.

6 Check the lengths of the sides of the triangle you have drawn by measuring.

7 Draw two more triangles with sides of the same lengths but make the base of one equal to **AC** and the base of the other equal to **BC**.

8 Cut out each of these triangles and fit them one on top of the other.

9 Measure in mm the sides of triangle **XYZ** and draw one exactly the same size.

10 Draw triangles each having sides of:
   a 120 mm, 80 mm, 60 mm
   b 85 mm, 70 mm, 65 mm
   c 57 mm, 73 mm, 112 mm.

11 Name the kind of triangles you have drawn according to
   a their sides      b their angles.

## B

Use a ruler and compasses to draw triangles with three equal sides each:

1  a 65 mm      b 90 mm      c 78 mm.

2 Name these triangles according to their sides.

3 Get a 60° set square, and by fitting it into the angles of the triangles, find the size of each angle.

4 Name these triangles according to their angles.

5 Each of these triangles has three lines of symmetry. Show them with dotted lines.

## C

Draw these triangles on a sheet of paper.

1  a base 85 mm, two equal sides of 70 mm
   b base 110 mm, two equal sides of 75 mm
   c base 98 mm, two equal sides of 52 mm

2 Name these triangles according to
   a their sides      b their angles.

3 Cut out each of the triangles you have drawn.
   Show, by folding, that the two angles at the base of each triangle are equal.

4 How many lines of symmetry has each triangle? Show them with dotted lines.

# Angles in shapes

## A

1 Copy the diagram. Use a set square to draw the line **AC** which is perpendicular to the line **AB**.

2 Join **BC** and measure it in cm.

3 You have drawn a right-angled triangle.
 a Mark the right angle *x*.
 b Write the lengths of its sides, putting the shortest first.

This special triangle was discovered many centuries ago, by the Egyptians, who used the right angle to help in building.
It is often called the **3, 4, 5** triangle.

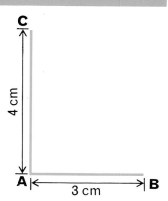

4 Draw another right-angled triangle with **AB**, 6 cm long, and the perpendicular **AC**, 8 cm long.

5 a Mark the right angle *x*.
 b Write the lengths of the sides, putting the shortest first.

6 Compare the lengths of the sides of each triangle. What do you discover?

7 Find the lengths of the sides of another right-angled triangle.
 Check the answer by drawing.

## B

**Remember** The sum of the three angles in any triangle is 2 right angles or 180°.

Find the measurement in degrees of the angle marked *x* in each triangle.

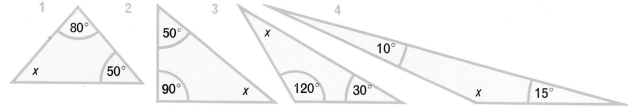

## C

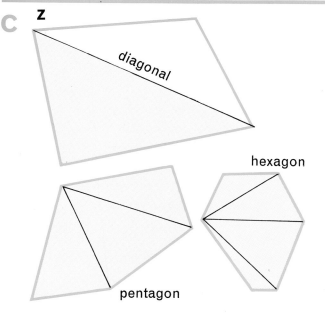

1 What is the name of the shape marked **Z**?

2 A diagonal has been drawn. Into how many triangles has the diagonal cut the shape?

3 How many right angles are equal to the sum of the three angles in each triangle?

4 How many a right angles b degrees are equal to the sum of the four angles in a quadrilateral?

5 How many a right angles b degrees are equal to the sum of the angles in
  a pentagon, 5 sides
  a hexagon, 6 sides?

6 Draw an octagon, 8 sides.
 a Into how many triangles can it be divided?
 b Find the sum of its angles in right angles and degrees.

# Solids   nets

## A

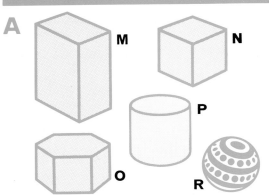

Look at the pictures of some common objects of different shapes. Collect at least one of each shape.

1   How many faces have shapes **M**, **N**, **O**, **P** and **R**?

2   The faces are either flat or curved. Writing the letters only, give the members of each of these sets.
F = { shapes with flat faces only }
C = { shapes with curved faces only }
B = { shapes with both curved and flat faces }

3   Which takes up more space:
a   an empty matchbox or a full one
b   a hollow ball or a solid ball of the same size?

> **Remember**   Shapes which take up space and have length, breadth and thickness (or height) are called **solids**. Some solids are hollow.

## B

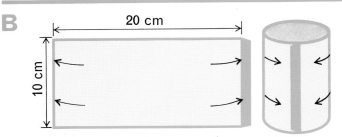

1   On a piece of thin card draw a rectangle 20 cm by 10 cm. Add a flap 5 mm wide. Cut it out.

2   Take the two edges, bring them together and fasten down the flap with gum.
You have made a hollow **cylinder**.

3   What is its  a  height  b  circumference?

4   What is the shape of the top and bottom?

## C

1   On a piece of thin card draw a rectangle 24 cm by 6 cm. Add a flap 5 mm wide. Cut it out.

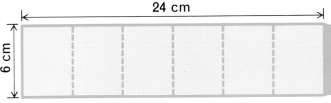

2   Divide it into six equal parts, as shown.

3   Bend the rectangle along the dotted lines to make a 6-sided shape and fasten down the flap with gum. You have made a hollow **hexagonal** solid.

4   What is the shape of the top and the bottom?

5   What is the height of the solid?

6   What is the shape of each face?

## D

The drawing shows another solid called a **sphere**.
A sphere has only one face which is curved.

1   Make a sphere from a lump of plasticine.

2   Using a pencil point, mark a line all round the sphere.
Note that the line comes back to the point from which it started.

3   Give a reason why a golf ball and a football are spheres.

4   Centuries ago, sailors believed that the earth was flat.
Give a reason why later they thought the earth was a sphere.

# Solids  volume

**A**

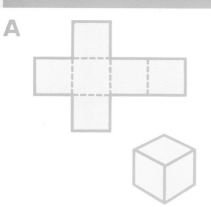

In **Beta Mathematics Book 2**, a **rectangular solid** (a cuboid) was made from a net.

1 Look at this net of a solid. How many faces has the solid?

2 What is the shape of each face?

3 On cm squared paper, copy the net. Draw the squares twice as large, but all the same size.

4 Cut out the net and fold the faces upwards along the dotted lines.
If you wish, you can fasten the edges with sellotape.

5 You have made a **cube**. What is:
a its length    b its width    c its height?

**B** The amount of space which a solid takes up is called its **volume**.

Volume is measured in cubes.

If the edges of a solid are measured in centimetres the volume is measured in **centimetre cubes** or **cubic centimetres (cm$^3$)**.

 **X**

The bar **X** is made by fitting together centimetre cubes.

1 Name the solid which is made.

2 How many centimetre cubes are there in the bar?

3 Write its volume in cm$^3$.

4 Find in cm   a its length    b its width
c its height or thickness.

**Y**

In drawing **Y**, two such bars are placed side by side.

5 Name the solid which is made.

6 How many centimetre cubes are there in the solid?

7 Write its volume in cm$^3$.

8 Find in cm   a its length    b its width
c its height or thickness.

9 Name the solid which is made if three bars, the same as **X**, are placed side by side.

10 How many centimetre cubes are there in the solid?

11 Write its volume in cm$^3$.

12 Find in cm   a its length    b its width
c its height or thickness.

13 Eight bars the same as **X** are placed side by side. Answer questions **9** to **12**.

14 Get 24 centimetre cubes.
Make two different cuboids each 1 cm thick.
Draw the solids you have made and write the length and width of each.

15 Using all the 24 centimetre cubes, build a cuboid which is 2 cm high.
Draw it and write its length and width.

16 Build a different cuboid 2 cm high.
Write its length and width.

# Test yourself   decimal notation, fractions

**A**

**1** Write and complete.

2600 = ☐ thousands ☐ hundreds
= ☐ hundreds

**2** 3064 = ☐ hundreds ☐ tens ☐ units
= ☐ tens ☐ units

Find the missing numbers.

**3** 3406 = 3000 + ☐ + 6

**4** 4170 = 4000 + 100 + ☐

Write the answers only.

**5** 972 + 30   **6** 1060 + 7   **7** 1305 + 900

**8** 407 − 50   **9** 1609 − 600   **10** 2004 − 90

Find the next numbers in these series.

**11** 800, 1300, 1800, ☐, ☐

**12** 850, 900, 950, ☐, ☐

**13** 2015, 2010, 2005, ☐, ☐

---

**B**

Write as decimal fractions.

**1** 6 units and 13 hundredths

**2** 40 units and 9 hundredths

**3** 104 tenths   **4** 7 hundredths

**5** 56 hundredths   **6** 304 hundredths

**7** Write the number shown on each abacus.

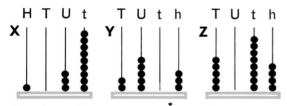

Draw an abacus picture to show:

**8** 5 tenths more than **X**

**9** 7 hundredths more than **Y**

**10** 20 hundredths more than **Z**.

Write the value of each digit underlined.

**11** 0.8<u>6</u>   **12** 47.1<u>5</u>   **13** 116.<u>2</u>

Write and complete the number series.

**14** 0.07, 0.7, 7, ☐, ☐   **15** 0.4, 4, 40, ☐, ☐

**16** How many times greater is   a   35 than 3.5
b   170 than 1.7   c   58 than 0.58?

**17** How many times less is   a   6.5 than 65
b   8.5 than 850   c   0.03 than 30?

---

**C**

Each shape **X**, **Y** and **Z** represents a whole one.

**1** What fraction of each whole one is
a   shaded   b   unshaded?

**2** Write each fraction in its lowest terms.

Write and complete:

**3** $\frac{2}{3} = \frac{\square}{6} = \frac{\square}{12} = \frac{\square}{24}$   **4** $\frac{3}{5} = \frac{\square}{10} = \frac{\square}{20} = \frac{\square}{100}$

**5** $\frac{7}{8} = \frac{\square}{16} = \frac{\square}{24} = \frac{\square}{40}$   **6** $\frac{7}{10} = \frac{\square}{50} = \frac{\square}{100}$

| | | | | |
|---|---|---|---|---|
| $\frac{8}{16}$ | $\frac{16}{20}$ | $\frac{25}{100}$ | $\frac{12}{18}$ | $\frac{70}{100}$ |
| $\frac{50}{100}$ | $\frac{40}{50}$ | $\frac{6}{24}$ | $\frac{20}{30}$ | $\frac{14}{20}$ |

Choose from the fractions in the box two which are equal to:

**7** $\frac{1}{2}$   **8** $\frac{1}{4}$   **9** $\frac{2}{3}$   **10** $\frac{4}{5}$   **11** $\frac{7}{10}$.

What fraction in its lowest terms is equal to:

**12** 3 out of 9   **13** 8 out of 20

**14** 6 out of 15   **15** 20 out of 25

**16** 30 out of 50   **17** 90 out of 100?

**18** $\frac{3}{4}$ of a number is 36. Find
a   $\frac{1}{4}$ of the number   b   all of the number.

In the same way, find all of the number when:

**19** $\frac{5}{6}$ is 35   **20** $\frac{9}{10}$ is 72

**21** $\frac{7}{8}$ is 42   **22** $\frac{3}{20}$ is 24.

Write as   a   improper fractions
b   mixed numbers.

**23** 17 quarters   **24** 59 tenths

**25** 23 fifths   **26** 41 sixths

Write the answers as decimals.

**27** $30 + 7 + \frac{9}{10}$   **28** $60 + 9 + \frac{34}{100}$

**29** $5 + \frac{4}{10} + \frac{3}{100}$   **30** $17 + \frac{4}{100}$

**31** $10 + \frac{9}{100}$   **32** $\frac{9}{10} + \frac{7}{100}$

Write these decimal fractions as vulgar fractions in their lowest terms.

**33** 0.6   **34** 1.75   **35** 1.25   **36** 3.15

# Test yourself money and measures

**A**

 £1·07   £0·53   57p    £1·20

1 Write these prices in order, largest first.

2 What is the difference between the largest and smallest price?

3 Find the total of all the prices.

How many

4 FIVES have the same value as:
  a 75p     b £0·95     c £1·85

5 TENS have the same value as:
  a £0·80     b £2·50     c £3·60?

6 What is the value of the figure underlined in each of these sums of money?
  a £0·6<u>4</u>     b £1·0<u>4</u>     c £1<u>3</u>·56

Find the change from:

7 1 FIFTY after spending   a 13p   b 28p

8 £1 after spending   a 74p   b 35p

9 £5 note after spending   a £1·80   b £3·46.

Find the totals of these notes and coins.

| £5 notes | £1 | 50p | 20p | 10p | 5p | 2p | 1p |
|---|---|---|---|---|---|---|---|
| | | 1 | 1 | | 1 | 2 | 1 |
| | 1 | 1 | 1 | 1 | | 4 | |
| | 1 | 2 | | | 4 | | 7 |
| 1 | 3 | | 2 | 3 | 2 | 3 | 2 |

Write the least number of notes and coins which make up these amounts.

14 29p     15 74p     16 £1·08

17 £3·40     18 £6·26     19 £10·64

Multiply each of these sums of money:

20 by 10    a 7p    b 56p    c £1·09

21 by 100.    a 3p    b 21p    c £0·74

Divide each of these sums of money:

22 by 10    a 90p    b £1·80    c £3·20

23 by 100.    a £6    b £19    c £150

**B**

M

N

O

P

1 Measure the lines **M, N, O** and **P** in mm.

2 Write the length of each
  a in cm    b to the nearest cm.

3 Use a straight edge to draw a line which you estimate is 20 cm long.
Measure the line and find out if your estimate is too long or too short.

4 What is the length of your span in cm? If you do not know, measure it.

5 Get a sheet from a newspaper. Estimate, by spanning, its length and width.

6 Measure to the nearest cm its length and width and find out if your estimates were too long or too short.

Work with a partner.
You will need a 10-metre tape.

7 In the playground, mark a starting line. From it walk forward 10 paces and mark the distance.

8 Estimate this distance in m. Measure it to the nearest m and find if your estimate was too long or too short.

9 From your measurements find the length of your pace in cm.

10 By pacing, estimate the shortest length and width of the playground.
Check your estimates by measuring.

11 By pacing, make estimates of other lengths and widths in the school.

# Test yourself money and measures

**A** Write these measurements in order of size, the greatest first.

1 17.3 cm, 170 mm, 1.80 m, 2 m

2 10 km, 9700 m, 10.050 km, 9.850 km

3 $2\frac{1}{2}$ kg, 2.450 kg, 2700 g, 2.6 kg

4 4 ℓ, 3950 mℓ, 4.050 ℓ, 4.1 ℓ

5 A map is drawn to scale of 5 mm to 1 km. How many km do lines of these lengths represent?
a 25 mm  b 3.5 cm  c 8.5 cm

The following lines are drawn to the given scales. Measure the lines and find their actual lengths.

6 1 cm to 10 m
—————————————————————————

7 1 mm to 5 cm
————————————————————

8 1 cm to 200 m
——————————————————————

9 1 cm to 50 km
—————————————————————

10 1 mm to 4 km
————————————————

11 ————————————————————————
The line represents a distance of $5\frac{1}{2}$ m. Measure the line and find to what scale it has been drawn.

The timetable gives the departure and arrival times of five trains from London to Leeds.

| London dep. | Leeds arr. |
|---|---|
| 07.50 | 10.37 |
| 11.25 | 13.58 |
| 15.55 | 18.25 |
| 17.04 | 19.56 |
| 19.40 | 22.51 |

12 Write in 12-hour clock times the departure and arrival times for each journey.

13 Find the time taken for each journey.

14 Which train was
a the fastest  b the slowest?

15 By how many degrees Celsius does the temperature fall from:
a 17°C to 9°C
b 13°C to 0°C  c 1°C to −5°C?

**B** Find the cost of these shopping items.

1 $1\frac{1}{2}$ m at 24p per m    2 10 ℓ at 84p per ℓ

3 $2\frac{1}{2}$ kg at 18p per kg    4 $1\frac{1}{4}$ kg at 60p per kg

5 $1\frac{1}{2}$ kg at 20p per $\frac{1}{2}$ kg    6 $\frac{3}{4}$ kg at 48p per $\frac{1}{2}$ kg

7 1 m of ribbon costs 40p. Find the cost of:
a 50 cm    b 10 cm    c 30 cm.

8 10 cm of cloth cost 36p. Find the cost of:
a 1 m    b $\frac{1}{4}$ m    c 70 cm.

Find the cost of these lengths.

9 10 cm at £2·80 per m

10 1 m 10 cm at £3·50 per m

11 60 cm at 70p per m

12 2 m 40 cm at £1·20 per m

13 3 m 90 cm at £2·50 per m

14 What fraction of 1 kg is:
a 500 g    b 750 g    c 100 g?

15 A method of reckoning quickly is to make a **ready reckoner**. Draw and complete this table.

| price per kg | 100 g | 200 g | 300 g | 400 g | 500 g | 600 g | 700 g | 800 g | 900 g |
|---|---|---|---|---|---|---|---|---|---|
| 70p | | | | | | | | | |
| £1·20 | | | | | | | | | |
| £4·00 | | | | | | | | | |

Check the completed ready reckoner from the answer book. Correct any mistakes. Use it to find the cost of these items.

16 700 g at £1·20 per kg    17 1 kg 200 g at 70p per kg    18 2 kg 100 g at 70p per kg

19 300 g at £4 per kg    20 1 kg 800 g at £1·20 per kg    21 2 kg 400 g at £4 per kg

# Test yourself   measures

**A** The picture shows a spring balance.

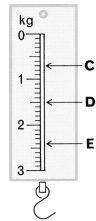

1 Using this balance, what is the greatest mass that can be weighed?

2 Write in g the mass represented by each small division on the scale.

3 Write in kg and g the mass shown by the pointers **C, D** and **E**.

4 Collect articles of different masses, e.g. parcels of books, paper, etc.
   Estimate which of them have a mass:
   a  less than 500 g
   b  between $\frac{1}{2}$ kg and 1 kg
   c  more than 1 kg.

5 Check your estimates by weighing on a suitable balance.

The picture shows a glass cylinder for measuring liquids. Look at the scale.

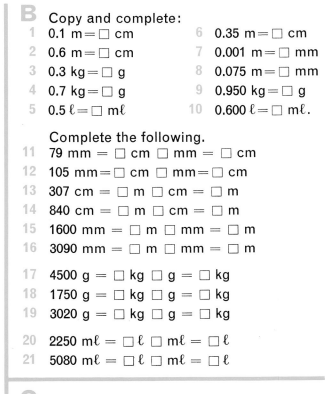

6 Using this measuring cylinder, what is the greatest amount of liquid which can be measured?

7 What fraction of 1 litre is this measure?

8 How many mℓ are represented by
   a  each large division
   b  each small division?

9 Find the amount of liquid in the measure shown by the pointers **Q** and **S**.

10 What decimal fraction of 1 litre is each?

11 Write the amounts of liquid shown by the pointers **R** and **T**.

12 Get the measures of capacity shown on page 57. Collect several containers which you estimate hold less than 1 litre, e.g. cups, jars, etc.
   Use the most suitable measure to find how many mℓ each container holds.

**B** Copy and complete:
1  0.1 m = ☐ cm
2  0.6 m = ☐ cm
3  0.3 kg = ☐ g
4  0.7 kg = ☐ g
5  0.5 ℓ = ☐ mℓ
6  0.35 m = ☐ cm
7  0.001 m = ☐ mm
8  0.075 m = ☐ mm
9  0.950 kg = ☐ g
10  0.600 ℓ = ☐ mℓ.

Complete the following.
11  79 mm = ☐ cm ☐ mm = ☐ cm
12  105 mm = ☐ cm ☐ mm = ☐ cm
13  307 cm = ☐ m ☐ cm = ☐ m
14  840 cm = ☐ m ☐ cm = ☐ m
15  1600 mm = ☐ m ☐ mm = ☐ m
16  3090 mm = ☐ m ☐ mm = ☐ m

17  4500 g = ☐ kg ☐ g = ☐ kg
18  1750 g = ☐ kg ☐ g = ☐ kg
19  3020 g = ☐ kg ☐ g = ☐ kg

20  2250 mℓ = ☐ ℓ ☐ mℓ = ☐ ℓ
21  5080 mℓ = ☐ ℓ ☐ mℓ = ☐ ℓ

**C** Change the following:
1  to mm    a  6.4 cm        b  20.7 cm
            c  2.480 m       d  5.375 m
2  to cm    a  3.8 m         b  1.74 m
            c  5.05 m        d  0.90 m
3  to g     a  4 kg 250 g    b  7 kg 620 g
            c  5.050 kg      d  2.390 kg
4  to mℓ.   a  3ℓ 400 mℓ     b  6ℓ 850 mℓ
            c  3.6 ℓ         d  8.250 ℓ

Find the difference between:
5  1 m and 39 cm
6  1 km and 700 m
7  370 g and 0.5 kg
8  0.45 m and 60 cm
9  0.4 ℓ and 1 ℓ
10  1 kg and 450 g.

11  Write to the nearest m.
    a  5 m 350 mm        b  3.860 m
12  Write to the nearest ℓ.
    a  14 ℓ 780 mℓ       b  49.250 ℓ
13  Write to the nearest $\frac{1}{2}$ kg.
    a  13 kg 650 g       b  20.920 kg

# Test yourself   shapes and space

## A

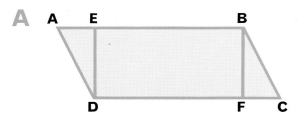

1 Name three different shapes in the diagram.

Name by letters:

2 the lines which are perpendicular to **DC**

3 the line which is parallel to
  a **AD**   b **DC**   c **BF**.

4 Use a ruler and set square to draw
  a a square of 5.5 cm side
  b a rectangle 8 cm long and 45 mm wide.

5 Draw a diagonal in each shape and measure it in mm.

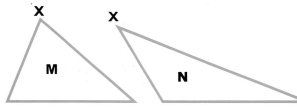

6 Measure in mm the sides of **M** and **N**.

7 Use the measurements to draw the two triangles.

8 In each triangle draw from **X** a line which is perpendicular to the base.

9 Measure in mm the height of each triangle.

10 Name them according to their angles.

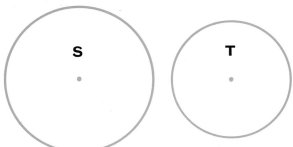

11 With a pair of compasses draw:
  a a circle which has twice the radius of **S**
  b a circle which has three times the diameter of **T**.

## B

1 Turns or rotations are measured in **degrees.** 1 complete turn measures ▱°.

2

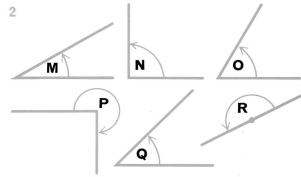

Write the letter of the angle which is:
90°,   60°,   30°,   45°,   180°,   270°.

3 What fraction of a complete turn is each of these angles?

4 Draw an 8-point compass card.

5 Through how many degrees does a boy turn clockwise from:
  a SE to W   b NW to S   c E to N?

6 Through how many degrees does he turn anticlockwise from:
  a SW to SE   b W to NE   c N to SW?

7 Through how many degrees does the minute-hand of a clock turn in 5 min?

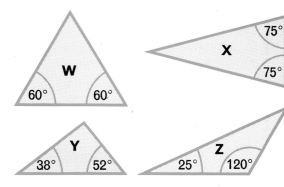

8 In each of the triangles **W, X, Y** and **Z**, find the number of degrees in the third angle.

9 Write the letter of the triangle which is:
  a equilateral   b isosceles
  c right-angled   d scalene.